EP BOOKS

1st Floor Venture House, 6 Silver C
Garden City, UK, AL7 1TS

http://www.epbooks.org

admin@epbooks.org

EP Books are distributed in the USA by:

JPL Distribution

3741 Linden Avenue Southeast

Grand Rapids, MI 49548

orders@jplbooks.com

© Joel Beeke 2017. All rights reserved. No part of this publication may be reproduced, stored in a retrieval system or transmitted, in any form, or by any means, electronic, mechanical, photocopying, recording or otherwise, without the prior permission of the publishers.

British Library Cataloguing in Publication Data available

ISBN 978-1-78397-192-3

Scripture quotations in this publication are from the The Holy Bible, King James Version.

How to Live as a Christian

Edited by

Joel Beeke

Contents

Preface	7
Coming to Christ	9
Union with Christ	12
Experiencing Justification and Adoption	15
Growing in Sanctification	18
Assured and Persevering	21
Reading the Scriptures	24
Why and How We Pray	27
Worship and the Means of Grace	30
Fellowship with Believers	33
How We Regard Ourselves	36
Love to God	39
The Fear of God	42
Living by the Ten Commandments	45
Godly Contentment	48
Self-Denial	51
Humility	54

How We Kill Pride	57
Coping with Criticism	60
Enduring Affliction	63
Spiritual Desertion	66
Fleeing Worldliness	69
Fighting against Backsliding	72
Family Worship	75
Being a Christ-like Husband	78
Being a Godly Wife	81
Showing Hospitality	84
Raising Children in the Lord	87
Being a Christian Grandparent	90
Honoring Your Parents	93
Serving God at Work	96
Using Leisure Time Well	99
Witnessing for Christ	102
Defending Our Faith	105
Facing Sickness and Death	108
Living Positively	111
Living for God's Glory	114

Preface

Reformed Christianity has long recognized that we exist to know God and to make His glory known through Jesus Christ for the eternal joy of His people. How do we do that in practical life?

The thirty-six brief articles collected in this book seek to answer that question in some of the beautiful variety of the Christian life. Here is a gem with many sparkling facets. For example, chapters address such facets of the Christian life as how to come to Christ for salvation, how to pray, what it means to love and fear God, how to flee worldliness and avoid backsliding, and what Christian faithfulness looks like as a child, parent, husband, wife, and grandparent. Written by godly Christians, these articles were published at the end of the Reformation Heritage KJV Study Bible and are now available in a slightly enlarged edition in this book.

I would like to thank the following persons who contributed to this book: Michael Barrett, James Beeke, Mary Beeke, Gerald Bilkes, Lawrence Bilkes, Brian DeVries, Bartel Elshout, Terreth Klaver, John Koopman, David Kranendonk, Ray Lanning, David Lipsy, Arthur Miskin, Eric Moerdyk, David Murray, Don Overbeek, Hans Overduin, Joel Overduin, Jon Payne, Ray Pennings, Cornelis Pronk, Johnny Serafini, Paul Smalley, Geoffrey Thomas, David VanBrugge, Pieter VanderMeyden, and William VanDoodewaard. The remainder of the articles were written by me, and I had the privilege of editing all the articles.

May the God of peace, who brought up our Lord Jesus Christ from the dead through the blood of the everlasting covenant, use this book powerfully to make its readers complete in every good work to do His will, working in us what is pleasing in His sight through Jesus Christ, to His glory forever! Amen.

Joel R. Beeke

How to Live as a Christian

Coming to Christ

Since the fall of man into sin, the great question has been: "How can sinners be brought back to God?" God drove Adam and Eve out of Paradise for their sins, but through Christ we can return to God and Paradise (Rev. 22:1–2). John therefore testifies, "And the Spirit and the bride say, Come. And let him that heareth say, Come. And let him that is athirst come. And whosoever will, let him take the water of life freely" (v. 17). Man was sent away from God, but now he is brought to God through Jesus Christ. The question that remains is: How do you and I come to Christ?

What does it mean to come to Christ? Mistaken views abound, such as making a decision for Christ in one's own strength, raising hands during silent prayer, reciting the sinner's prayer, walking forward during an altar call, getting baptized, taking the Lord's Supper, mentally agreeing to certain truths, having mystical experiences, or seeing miracles.

Coming to Christ begins with God's call. God commands all who hear the gospel to repent and trust in Christ. The gospel presents Christ to men for their salvation. Paul said, "But we preach Christ crucified.... Christ the power of God, and the wisdom of God" (1 Cor. 1:23–24). The death and resurrection of the Son of God are powerful to save sinners. Christ says, "Come unto me all ye that labor and are heavy laden, and I will give you rest" (Matt. 11:28). When someone refuses to come to Him, all blame rests upon the sinner. Jesus said, "Ye will not come to me, that ye might have life" (John 5:40).

However, God does more than issue a universal call. He also makes an effectual call that draws sinners to Christ. The Lord Jesus said, "All that the Father giveth me shall come to me; and him that cometh to me I will in no wise cast out" (John 6:37). We are so blind and dead in sin (Eph. 2:1; 2 Cor. 4:4) that we cannot come and will not come, but with God all things are possible (Matt. 19:26; John 6:44; Eph. 2:5).

We come to Christ when we are drawn actively to Him by faith as He offers Himself to sinners in the gospel through the power of the Holy Spirit. Such faith involves self-renunciation as we see we have no righteousness of our own (Phil. 3:9), reliance as we rest upon Christ's person and shed blood upon the cross (Rom. 3:25), and appropriation as we receive Christ and apply Him as the great medicine for all our spiritual needs (John 1:12). We can only come to Christ to save us from sin if we see ourselves as sinners, breakers of God's holy law who deserve judgment (Rom. 3:19–20).

By the Spirit's grace, have you turned in faith to Christ as He is offered in the gospel as your only hope for salvation? This is a sure sign of coming to Him! If this is so, give glory to God, for apart from the Holy Spirit no one can come to Christ (1 Cor. 12:3). The Spirit gives life, and the flesh profits nothing (John 6:63). Praise the Father that His Spirit has blessed you with faith in Jesus Christ.

If you have not come to Christ, then why not? Let no obstacle hinder you. Read the Bible and listen to preaching that testifies of Christ. Don't let friends lead you astray. Do not let the sins of people in church keep you back from eternal life. If you have not already, learn the basics of Christianity through a good catechism. Do not persist in unbelief or harden your heart. Stop loving this world. Quit clinging to your sins. Repent and believe the gospel. Don't be a fool and think that God would never damn you. On the other hand, do not be so proud as to think that your sins are greater than the grace of Christ. Christ can save the worst of sinners. Do not delay. Humble yourself today, and call upon the name of the Lord Jesus. He is rich to save all who come to Him.

Union with Christ

Union with Christ is undoubtedly one of the most extraordinary blessings and privileges of every Christian. That union is forged by the Holy Spirit in the hour of regeneration when He cuts a sinner off from Adam and grafts him into Christ. The Spirit then establishes a spiritual union between Christ and the sinner—a union that is unbreakable, irreversible, and eternal.

In so doing, the Holy Spirit reestablishes a covenantal relationship between God and sinners that once existed between God and Adam prior to the Fall. Though the essence of this union is identical to this original covenantal union, one difference is significant: the covenant bond between God and Adam proved to be breakable because it was established externally from God's being. But when the Holy Spirit unites a sinner to Christ, the bond is internal to God's being. It lies within the second Person of the Godhead, the Lord Jesus Christ. When a sinner is united to Christ, he is thereby united to the triune God with a covenantal bond that cannot be severed to all eternity. As impossible as it is to sever the divine and human natures of Christ, so the covenantal bond between God and His people, established in Christ, can never be dissolved. Paul could therefore write boldly to believers that nothing "shall be able to separate us from the love of God, which is in Christ Jesus our Lord" (Rom. 8:39).

All of this is implied when we say that believers are united to Christ by faith. However, this glorious objective truth must also become an experiential reality for us if we are to enjoy its blessed benefits. Objectively, this union is established in the hour of regeneration, but this union with Christ is subjectively established and maintained by the exercise of faith. Only by faith can the believer become conscious of this union and enjoy its benefits.

Though from God's side this union is uninterrupted, from the believer's side the awareness and enjoyment of this union is very much contingent upon the exercise of faith. The more a believer exercises faith, the more he will enjoy the reality and comfort of being united to Christ. Enjoying this union is therefore directly proportionate to our believing appropriation of it. In John 15, Christ lovingly urges His people to abide in Him, saying, "Abide in me, and I in you.... I am the vine, ye are the branches: he that abideth in me, and I in him, the same bringeth forth much fruit" (John 15:4–5). Christ makes it abundantly clear that He desires believers to live in the full awareness and comfort of this union. It is therefore essential that believers exercise faith in the Lord Jesus Christ and His finished work each day afresh. There will be times that such faith is exercised when we are not engaged emotionally—and thus even in the absence of the sweet and tender frames God's children so much enjoy. At such moments we do not feel united to Christ, but by faith we embrace the truth that nevertheless we are united to Christ. What a blessing when we increasingly live by faith and not by feeling! "Faith is the substance of things hoped for, the evidence of things not seen" (Heb. 11:1).

Do you know whether you are united to this precious Christ? If you are, you will be irresistibly drawn to Christ, embrace Him by faith, be progressively conformed to Him, and be increasingly assured of your union with Him. If this in some measure is descriptive of your life, continue coming to and abiding in Christ. In so doing, you will increasingly enjoy your objective union with Christ and the more you will understand what Paul means when he writes, "There is therefore now no condemnation to them which are in Christ Jesus" (Rom. 8:1).

Experiencing Justification and Adoption

John Calvin once said that justification is the main hinge on which religion turns. According to him, "justified by faith is he who, excluded from the righteousness of works, grasps the righteousness of Christ through faith, and clothed in it, appears in God's sight not as a sinner but as a righteous man." We find echoes of this definition of justification in Lord's Day 23 of the Heidelberg Catechism when it speaks of God imputing "to me the perfect satisfaction, righteousness and holiness of Christ;...as if I never had had, nor committed any sin,...as if I had fully accomplished all that obedience which Christ has accomplished for me."

Yet, glorious as the doctrine of justification is, there is another, related doctrine, which is even more glorious: those who are justified by faith are also adopted by God as members of His family. Why is this a greater blessing than the one flowing from justification? Adoption brings us into an even richer relationship with God than justification. Justification has to do with our legal relationship to God. In justification, God as Judge declares the sinner who believes in Christ free from the demands of the law because those demands have been met by another Surety. In adoption, however, God is not only our pacified Judge but our reconciled Father. This is the supreme good of the Christian religion. "Behold," says John the apostle, "what manner of love the Father has bestowed on us, that we should be called the sons of God" (1 John 3:1).

Why is this superior blessing not experienced more often in its richness by us? Why do not more believers enjoy the privileges of sonship as they should? Why do so many feel constrained to say with John Newton:

'Tis a point I long to know,
Oft it causes anxious thought,
Do I love the Lord or no?
Am I His or am I not?

There are valid reasons for such laments. Most of God's people have times when fears and doubts beset them. When they realize who and what they are before a holy God, they can find it difficult to appropriate such great blessings to themselves. They may possess the essential marks of grace and yet often hesitate to say, "Abba, Father!" They may believe that Christ is their only hope and refuge and there are times "when peace like a river attends [their] way," but they can also go through periods when they do not have the full assurance of their sonship as they wish.

Am I describing your case? Do you often lack boldness to approach God with full assurance as your Father? So what do you do? You must learn to fix your mind on this truth: children of God are adopted through grace, for Christ's sake. Our sonship grows out of Christ's Sonship! It is based on what He has done to earn the blessing of sonship for us. He was rejected by God for a time and so deprived of His Father's love that He cried out, "My God"—not my Father, but my God—"why hast thou forsaken me?" He did this in order "that we might be accepted of God and never be forsaken of Him" (Form for Administration of the Lord's Supper).

How marvelous is God's way of salvation! Does your heart burn within you when you hear these wonderful truths of the Word of God (Luke 24:32)? Are you still afraid to call God your Father, even if you cannot deny that you believe on His Son? Your Father wants you to call Him by His rightful name. When the prodigal son returned to his father's house with a repentant heart, he was no doubt afraid that he would find the door to that house closed. Having sinned against heaven and his father, he could not expect to be received as a son. But his father had other plans for him. Picture the scene: the father running toward his long-lost son, followed by a hearty embrace and ardent kiss, then the best robe, the ring, the shoes, and the feast—and all for a son who had been dead but was alive again.

Growing in Sanctification

It is safe to say that the major concern the apostles had for the lives of those under their care was that they should live holy lives (1 Thess. 5:23; 1 Peter 1:15; 1 John 1:5–6). Sanctification is so critical that professing believers who have no desire for it reveal the dangerous state of their soul, for without holiness no one will see the Lord (Heb. 12:14).

To know how to live a sanctified life, therefore, must be a top priority for the Christian. How are we sanctified?

First, we must know and trust in the triune God who saves people from sin. Sanctification is, very simply, to grow in the likeness of our God and Father. By conforming to the image of Christ, we inevitably become more like God. One must begin by trusting Christ's finished work on the cross whereby His people are saved and made able to be sanctified. Without His life and death, there would be no justification and therefore no sanctification. The Holy Spirit indwells and sanctifies us by making us alive, giving us a heart for the things of God, applying the Word to our hearts, and creating His fruit in our lives. Without the triune God, we would all be relinquished to our natural state of being dead in our sins and trespasses, in the grips of a threefold enemy: Satan, the world, and indwelling sin (Eph. 2:1–2).

Second, we must trust that God has given us, in His Word and specifically in the Ten Commandments, all we need to know about holiness. The Bible contains what we must repent of as well as what we must obey—what we must stop doing, thinking, and feeling, and what we must begin doing, thinking, and feeling (Isa. 1:16–17; Rom. 13:12; Eph. 4:22, 24).

Third, we must be assured that God has given all the power necessary for sanctification to take place in the life of His children. In Ephesians 1:16-20, Paul prays that they would know God, have hope, know the riches of the glory of their inheritance, and know the exceeding greatness of God's power toward believers. Then he proceeds to explain that this mighty power is the very power with which Jesus was raised from the dead and "set him at his own right hand in the heavenly places" (Eph. 1:17-20).

Fourth, we must guard against two great errors regarding sanctification: legalism and liberalism. Legalism seeks to add the merit of our works to Christ and the wisdom of our rules to God's Word, but in so doing it loses Christ, freedom, hope, obedience, grace, and love (Gal. 5:1-7). Liberalism twists our freedom in Christ into an opportunity for sin, leading to sexual immorality, false worship, strife in relationships, and lack of self-control (Gal. 5:13, 19-21).

Finally, we must be crucifying the flesh and living in the Spirit (Gal. 5:24-25). Crucifying the flesh is actively putting off sin and developing a greater and greater hatred of sin. Sin seeks to do nothing else but destroy any likeness of Christ. Therefore repentance is an ongoing grace—always confessing, praying for forgiveness, and turning from sin. Living in the Spirit is growing in holiness. It is to become more and more like Christ. The fruit of the Spirit are graces diametrically opposite to the works of the flesh (Gal. 5:22-23). Love would exterminate adultery, hatred, strife, and envy. Temperance is a powerful weapon against uncleanness, drunkenness, and revelings; meekness against murders; peace against seditions, and goodness against wrath. These are graces that do not originate in the human heart. They are a direct consequence of the indwelling of the Spirit.

Christians are recipients of grace, yet fully responsible to obey the command to trust the Lord and diligently make use of spiritual disciplines—Scripture reading and meditation, prayer, the preached Word and sacraments, fellowship with believers, the reading of orthodox literature, the evangelization of others, etc.—in order to have such fruit produced in abundance in our lives.

Thus, we can understand our dire need of the triune God, His holy Word, and His powerful hand, that He may graciously lead us in the grace of sanctification, keeping us far from the dangerous rocks of legalism and precipices of liberalism—all to God's glory.

Assured and Persevering

The fruits of genuine assurance and perseverance are sorely lacking among Christians today. The fruits of assurance and perseverance—diligent use of the means of grace, heartfelt obedience to God's will, desire for fellowship with Him, yearning for His glory and heaven, love for the church, and intercession for revival—all appear to be waning. We desperately need rich, doctrinal thinking about assurance and perseverance coupled with vibrant, sanctified living.

What is "assurance of faith" and what is "perseverance of the saints" and how do we obtain them? How do assurance and perseverance assist each other in the Christian life?

Assurance of faith is the conviction that, by God's grace, I belong to Christ, have received full pardon for all sins, and will inherit eternal life (1 John 5:11–13). If I have true assurance, I not only believe in Christ for salvation but also know that I believe. Such assurance includes freedom from guilt, joy in God, and a sense of belonging to the family of God. Assurance is also dynamic, varying according to conditions, capable of growing in force and fruitfulness.

Assurance is obtained (1) by clinging to the promises of God (2 Cor. 7:1), (2) by the Spirit's confirmation of the marks and fruits of grace within us (1 John 4:7, 13), (3) by the direct testimony of the Spirit witnessing with our spirit that we are the children of God (Rom. 8:16), and (4) by resting in God's outstanding track record of faithfulness toward us (1 Thess. 5:23–24).

What is the perseverance of the saints? We first must ask, who are the saints? Many would extend "eternal security" to all baptized persons, or to all who have made decisions for Christ at evangelistic meetings. Scripture speaks only of the perseverance of saints (Jer. 32:40; Rom. 8:30, 37–39; Phil. 1:1, 6), defined as those "whom God calls, according to his purpose, to the communion of his Son, our Lord Jesus Christ, and regenerates by the Holy Spirit" (Canons of Dort, Fifth Head, Art. 1). By the preserving work of the triune God (1 Cor. 1:2, 8–9), such people will persevere in true faith and in the works that proceed from faith, as long as they continue in the world.

Some theologians want to speak of the preservation of the saints rather than perseverance. These two notions are closely related, but not the same. The preserving activity of God undergirds the saints' perseverance. He keeps them in the faith, preserves them from straying, and ultimately perfects them (1 Peter 1:5; Jude 24). We may be confident that God will finish the work of grace He has begun in us (Ps. 138:8; Phil. 1:6; Heb. 12:2). Believers are preserved through Christ's intercession (Luke 22:32; John 17:5) and the ministry of the Holy Spirit (John 14:16; 1 John 2:27).

Perseverance itself, however, is the saints' lifelong activity: confessing Christ as Savior (Rom. 10:9), bringing forth the fruits of grace (John 15:16), enduring to the end (Matt. 10:22; Heb. 10:28, 29). True believers persevere in the "things that accompany salvation" (Heb. 6:9). God does not deal with them "as unaccountable automatons, but as moral agents," says A. W. Pink; believers are active in sanctification (Phil. 2:12). They keep themselves from sin (1 John 5:18). They keep themselves in the love of God (Jude 21). They run with patience the race that is set before them (Heb. 12:1). That is how they persevere, and they are aided in this by the Holy Spirit.

How are assurance and perseverance related? Assurance helps the believer persevere, first, by encouraging him to rest on God's grace in Christ and His promises in the gospel; and second, by presenting these as a powerful motive for Christian living. Perseverance opens the way for assurance. If a man does not believe in the perseverance of the saints, he cannot be sure he is going to heaven. He may know he is in a state of grace, but he has no way of knowing whether or not he will continue in that state. Thus assurance is wedded to the doctrine of perseverance. Those who persist in doing the works that spring from faith will usually attain high levels of assurance over a period of time.

Reading the Scriptures

Effective Bible study is largely a matter of good work habits. Begin with firm determination; begin at once. Never wait until you are in the mood, or you may wait for weeks. Get in the mood by starting; the Bible creates its own mood. As J. C. Ryle says about it, "The way to do a thing is to do it." The way to read the Bible is actually to read it—not wishing and meaning and resolving and intending and thinking about reading the Bible, but actually reading it. You will not advance one step until you have done that.

If you have a plan to guide you, then you have a head start. Indeed, if you do not have a plan you will never read the Bible. You may read parts, but never the whole Book, and you will never gain that familiarity with it which is so necessary if you are to benefit from the fullness of its message.

There are various plans which, if followed, will take you through the whole Bible in a year, or even the Old Testament once in a year and through the New Testament and Psalms twice. They are ambitious programs of reading which require reading at least three or four chapters a day.

To follow such schemes is an ideal for a believer. It is true that there have been more ambitious goals attempted and attained. Samuel Annesley, John Wesley's grandfather, as a child of five or six began to read twenty chapters a day and continued that throughout his life. Arthur Pink wrote to a friend, "In my early years...I read through the entire Bible three times a year (eight chapters in the Old Testament and two in the New Testament daily). I steadily persevered in this for ten years in order to familiarize myself with its contents, which can only be done by consecutive reading." Few Christians today have that stamina.

Reading the Bible at the table after a meal is a wonderful habit; it should be the goal for every family. To make the most of it, each person should have a Bible open before him. In that way, one's thoughts can be prevented from wandering and everyone can join in the discussion after the passage is read. Such comments are necessary if the main thrust of the passage is to be understood by all present.

C. H. Spurgeon suggested, "Every minister ought to read Matthew Henry entirely and carefully through once at least. I should recommend you to get through it in the next twelve months after you leave college. Begin at the beginning and resolve that you will traverse the goodly land from Dan to Beersheba."

The chief aim of studying the Scriptures is not the amount read or even the reading itself. The aim is to know God. It is not to pacify our consciences that we are obeying our minister's exhortations and reading the Scriptures. Yet encouragements to persevere in reading can help, especially in the initial stages. For example, a congregation could adopt a scheme and distribute an outline throughout the membership. One of the readings in the Sunday service could be the set chapter for the day, at least in the first months.

In whatever ways we adapt the suggested plan to our own particular needs, aim at reading two or three chapters at a sitting, or a whole book or epistle. There are many precious things we shall never see unless we read the Word of God in chunks. We would never read fifteen lines of any other piece of literature and then set it aside, believing that we had satisfied the author's original intentions. To see the whole massive movement of biblical thought, the Scriptures need to be read frequently and from Genesis to Revelation. The Christian must be content with nothing less. He will not understand the individual verses unless he has the framework of knowledge which a larger acquaintance with Scripture provides. The more he reads, the more comprehensible the Bible becomes.

Why and How We Pray

"Lord, teach us to pray" (Luke 11:1). These words spoken by the disciples to the Lord Jesus Christ are revealing. It was customary in those days for rabbis to teach their disciples this important discipline. Yet there is more to this request than rabbinical custom. The disciples had heard Jesus pray various times; surely they were impressed and moved by the intimate bond with God that Jesus' prayers revealed, among other things in calling upon Him as Father.

Prayer is both the greatest privilege and greatest burden of every true Christian. It is a privilege because we can point to various times in our lives when prayer has been one of our greatest delights. You pour out your heart to God when burdened with sin, suffering, or need, and sense a living connection with Him. You want to say at such times like Jacob at Peniel, "This is none other but the house of God, the gate of heaven" (Gen. 28:17).

Other times you pray out of a sense of custom and obligation, and your prayers seem like empty repetitions and cold husks nearly devoid of life. You know something is wrong but are not quite sure what to do about it. If your prayers make you sigh, what effect do they have on God, you wonder. One reason we find prayer so difficult is that we tend to use the identical words to pray for the same things. Certainly there are always some new things to bring to the Lord, such as the crisis of the moment in the church or family. But most of our prayers are about the same things. It quickly seems boring and unspiritual.

There can also be the sneaking suspicion of unbelief in our hearts that wonders if prayer really accomplishes all that much. Remember the prayer meeting asking the Lord to free the apostle Peter from prison the night before his scheduled execution? When informed he was standing at the door, they said to the servant girl Rhoda, "You are mad" (Acts 12:15).

In light of these difficulties and struggles, it is important to realize that why we pray is the key to knowing how to pray. Why pray? The answer is simple, and yet profound and encouraging. As a father, I already know what my wife and children have planned for the day. Yet when I come home, I still ask what they did that day. I still listen to the childlike babbling of my toddlers with interest and delight. Just a few days ago, I took one of my toddlers on a bike ride. She pointed out every bird and animal she saw. I reacted with enthusiasm and enjoyed the interaction with my daughter. A father loves to interact with his children.

God becomes your Father through faith in Christ and the adoption of His grace (Gal. 4:4-6). Even when you feel cold or distant, God is the perfect Father who loves living interaction with His children. As earthly fathers, we become impatient, weary, or distracted. God the Father never suffers from such weaknesses (Matt. 7:11). Through Christ the Mediator, He also purifies our prayers so that they all rise accepted before Him like incense, even when we are most burdened by our coldness or weakness. Reminding yourself of this is a great help for prayer.

God has also given wonderful helps in how to pray. Have you ever wondered how someone could pray for an hour or more in a day? You feel unspiritual and second rate because you doubt you could ever do it. The secret is to pray God's own words back to Him. One method is to divide the Psalms into five sections of thirty each. So on the first day of the month, read Psalm 1, 31, 61, etc. Prompt yourself to pray over one verse or one thought at a time. Ask God to keep you meditating on His Word day and night. Perhaps at least one of the five Psalms of the day will prompt the fountains of prayer; you might not even get to them all before your time is up. You will find a freshness and variety to your prayers in so doing. The ACTS acronym—adoration, confession, thanksgiving, supplication—can also be a wonderful help to prayer. Adore God for who He is, confess your sins wholeheartedly, thank Him sincerely, and offer up your supplications to Him. He will hear the needy when they cry.

Finally, strive to take hold of both God (Isa. 64:7) and yourself (1 Thess. 5:17) when praying. Take hold of God by exercising faith in His Son, by looking to the glorious Trinity in prayer, by developing a right heart toward God in prayer, by bringing God His own Word and promises in prayer, by believing that God hears and answers prayer, by resting with contentment in God's all-sufficiency in prayer, and by seeking God's glory in prayer. Take hold of yourself by treasuring the value of prayer, maintaining the priority of prayer, speaking with sincerity in prayer, cultivating continual prayer, committing to intercessory prayer, and using the Bible as your guide in prayer.

Worship and the Means of Grace

When Christians assemble for worship on the Lord's Day, they participate in what is by far the most meaningful and consequential activity in the body of Christ. Worship is the highest calling of the believer. It is the center jewel on the crown of Christian discipleship. It is the verdant pasture in which Christ Jesus, the Good Shepherd, feeds and nourishes His sheep. Worship is the dynamic spiritual context in which the powers of the age to come break forth into this present evil age (Heb. 6:5; Gal. 1:4). Indeed, through the means of Word, sacraments, and prayer God is glorified and His children through faith gratefully receive the benefits of redemption in Christ (Westminster Larger Catechism, Q. 154). Therefore, it is paramount that we understand and devote ourselves to corporate worship on the Lord's Day.

The early Christians made public worship a priority in their lives. Luke reports that "they continued steadfastly in the apostles' doctrine and fellowship, and in breaking of bread, and in prayers" (Acts 2:42). Notice the definite article preceding each action; this indicates that this was public worship. And what constitutes worship in the nascent days of the church? The Word of God, the sacraments, and prayer (cf. Matt. 28:18–20).

The faithful reading and preaching of God's Word are essential to biblical worship. Paul writes to Timothy, "Till I come, give attendance to reading, to exhortation, to doctrine" (1 Tim. 4:13). Later he charges Timothy to "preach the word; be instant in season, out of season; reprove, rebuke, exhort with all longsuffering and doctrine" (2 Tim. 4:2). All pastors and churches are called to do the same—

without exception. The bride of Christ hears the voice of her beloved in worship when His living Word is read, and especially when it is preached (Rom. 10:17; Heb. 4:12). The Bible is the sure Word that we do well to pay attention to until Christ's return (2 Pet. 1:19–21; 1 Tim. 3:16–17).

The question is, dear believer, are you listening? Are you attending Lord's Day worship with a humble and teachable heart? Puritan George Swinnock commented that "all in the church may hear the Word of Christ, but few hear Christ in the Word." Nothing glorifies God more than when His dependent children gather together under the public ministry of the Word in order to hear, believe, and delight in His sublime attributes, loving promises, and fatherly commands. Moreover, nothing provides greater spiritual blessing for Christ's church (cf. Westminster Larger Catechism, Q. 155).

The sacraments of baptism and the Lord's Supper are also integral to biblical worship. They are signs and seals of God's covenant promises fulfilled in Christ. The waters of baptism represent Christ's cleansing blood and the regeneration of the Holy Spirit (Acts 22:16; Titus 3:5), and the bread and the wine of communion signify the broken body and shed blood of Christ—the sinless Lamb who bore God's wrath in our place (Matt. 26:26–28). Through these visible signs and seals, the Holy Spirit powerfully assures us that God "grants us freely the remission of sin and life eternal for the sake of that one sacrifice of Christ accomplished on the cross" (Heidelberg Catechism, Q. 66).

God creates and nourishes faith through the preaching of the Word, and He confirms it in the sacraments. Prayer, the third non-negotiable of biblical worship, is the church's humble and grateful response to the gospel (Ps. 103:1–5). Led by the minister or elders, prayer in worship is the church's heartfelt response (spoken or sung) to the sovereign majesty and grace of God.

Lord's Day worship is no ordinary activity. In an extraordinary way, biblical worship both glorifies God and sanctifies the believer. Therefore, on the divinely appointed "market day of the soul," faithfully attend worship with a ready heart and expectant faith (Heb. 10:25). Come with a heart that is eager and willing to exalt the name of the Lord and to joyfully receive all the spiritual benefits that your heavenly Father offers you in Christ.

Fellowship with Believers

John writes, "But if we walk in the light, as he is in the light, we have fellowship one with another" (1 John 1:3). Fellowship with other believers is a rich privilege and an important responsibility. Without it, our life would no doubt be very lonely and oppressive. Our fall into sin has cut us off from fellowship with God and godly fellowship with others; before God's work of grace in our hearts, we instead have "fellowship with the unfruitful works of darkness" (Eph. 5:11). But if in sovereign mercy God has engrafted you into His Son, you have begun to enjoy fellowship with Him and, through Him, with others.

The Bible frequently encourages and directs believers to fellowship. From this we can learn that God highly prizes the exercise of this grace for the comfort and growth of faith. Reflect on the following practical ways in which the Bible instructs believers to enjoy fellowship with each other:

1. By assembling with one another. This is the chief way Christians can enjoy fellowship. It's humbling to think that God has to warn us not to forsake such assemblies (Heb. 10:25). If Christians are providentially hindered from participating in corporate worship for a long time, it can be a great burden. Think of how sadness filled David's heart when he was remembering the day when he could go to the house of the Lord (Ps. 42:4).

2. By cultivating and displaying a gracious spirit towards each other. We cannot properly fellowship with each other when we are proud and self-centered. The Lord instructs us to show humility, gentleness, and patience towards each other (Eph. 4:1–3; 5:21). This often goes

against our nature, but a gracious spirit is conducive to fellowship.

3. By holy conversation with each other. Christians from the past seem to have been better at this than we in our busy and digitally-oriented society. Bunyan's *Pilgrim's Progress* shows many instances in which Christian was helped by spiritual conversations with fellow-travelers to the Celestial City. God promises rich blessings upon those who cultivate such spiritually-minded fellowship (Mal. 3:16–17).

4. By singing with each other. Singing can greatly aid the fellowship of kindred minds (Col. 3:16). This happens in corporate worship, family worship, or just informal gatherings.

5. By avoiding fellowship with unrighteousness. Fellowship with ungodly people is a sure way to undermine fellowship between believers. Believers cannot afford to change like chameleons depending on whose company they are in. The Bible warns believers not to fellowship with the ungodly (Ps. 1:1; Eph. 5:11; 2 Cor. 6:1–17).

6. By celebrating the Lord's Supper. The Lord's Supper serves a number of purposes. An important one is that believers would be united in brotherly love through the Spirit (1 Cor. 10:17).

7. By encouraging and helping each other. We should see times of difficulty as special calls to fellowship with each other. Scripture tells us that if one member of the body of Christ suffers, everyone else should feel it and seek to help as able (1 Cor. 12:26–27; Rom. 12:15). Sometimes this will mean a word of encouragement or sympathy. Other times,

contributing tangible help and resources is a beautiful expression of fellowship (2 Cor. 9:12–14).

8. By praying for each other. Can people still fellowship with each other when they are not physically together? On his many journeys and during imprisonment, Paul still enjoyed fellowship through prayer and thanksgiving for others (2 Cor. 1:11; Eph. 6:18). In a similar vein, Christians are called to cultivate fellowship with those who are persecuted by remembering them in prayer (Heb. 13:3).

Are you united to Christ? You cannot enjoy true fellowship with any of Christ's people without being united to Christ. If you are a child of God but are lax in your fellowship with other believers, examine what the cause might be. Are you humble, patient, and longing to serve others? Do you cultivate spiritual friendships? Do you use the means of grace prayerfully with a desire to be used for the good of others? In these times when the love of many is waxing cold, may God grow believers to exercise and enjoy deeper fellowship with Him and with each other.

How We Regard Ourselves

Right thinking about the gospel produces right living in the gospel. Vibrant Christianity does not exist in a mental vacuum; we must think right about God, about Christ, and about ourselves. In many ways, what we think about ourselves is the link between what we know to be true about the gospel and how we apply that to daily life. Simply said, how we regard ourselves is crucial to our sanctification, which is the effect of the gospel in our daily experience. The sad truth is that in our battle against sin we are too often our own worst enemy. The battle tends to rage most fiercely inside.

Romans 6 is a high-water text regarding the theology and procedure of sanctification. Significantly, Paul outlines three crucial steps in the process: what to know, how to behave, what to reckon. We are to know our union with Christ both in terms of His death and resurrection; union with Christ is our source of life (vv. 3-10). We are to behave by not letting sin rule and not yielding to sin's dominion (vv. 12-13). What we are to reckon puts the two together: "reckon ye also yourselves to be dead indeed unto sin, but alive unto God through Jesus Christ our Lord" (v. 11). Self-perception or how we view ourselves flows from what we know and leads to how we behave. Right thinking produces right living.

The verb "to reckon" is most suggestive. Our English word "logic" comes from this word, and the Greek verb means "to take into account," "to consider," or "to regard" something as true. The word emphasizes the vital appropriation of what is believed. What the Christian is to reckon is the same thing he is to believe: deadness to sin through union with Christ (v. 8). We must acknowledge the personal relevance of the truth. We must consider ourselves to be in experience what we are positionally and legally in Christ. The believer must never lose sight or thought of what he is and what he has in the Lord Jesus Christ.

Most remarkable is the fact that this word "reckon," so crucial to the process of sanctification, occurs also in connection with the doctrine of justification (Rom. 4:3-4). However, there is one difference. In justification, God is the subject of the verb. He looks at the merits of Christ's atonement and considers (reckons) the sinner who believes in Christ to be legally free from sin, no longer liable to penalty or condemnation, and positively clothed in the robe of Christ's righteousness. In sanctification, the saint is the subject of the verb. We look at the same merits of Christ's atonement and consider (reckon) ourselves to be free from the dominion of sin. Compare closely what we know about Christ in verses 9-10 (His irreversible resurrection, His emancipation from death, His living unto God) with what we are to reckon to ourselves (our death to sin and life unto God). What is true about Christ, we claim for ourselves. In other words, we are to regard ourselves the same way God regards us: in Christ.

How we see ourselves, then, is nothing more than thinking about the gospel and living in its reality. In Christ, we are united to both His death and His resurrection (v. 5). Regarding ourselves as God regards us means that we must factor into our constant experience the knowledge that when Christ died, we died. We must factor into our experience the purpose of the crucifixion: to put to death the "old man" with its bent to sin. We must factor into our experience the new life that we have in Christ with its bent toward holiness that frees us from having to sin.

To regard ourselves in union with Christ is the secret to sanctification and victory over sin. Sin loses its appeal in the shadow of the cross. How can it be attractive when we realize that sin is the reason Christ died for us and that we died with Him? We certainly are not to think more highly of ourselves than we ought to think, but we are to think "as God hath dealt to every man the measure of faith" (Rom. 12:3). It is by that faith that we see ourselves in Christ. That is right thinking.

Love to God

Deuteronomy 6:4–5 says, "Hear, O Israel: The LORD our God is one LORD: and thou shalt love the LORD thy God with all thine heart, and with all thy soul, and with all thy might." Our Lord and great Prophet told us that this is the first and greatest commandment (Mark 12:29). Deuteronomy 6 calls us to turn from all other gods and give sole allegiance to the Lord, because He is the "one" God, and "there is none else" (Deut. 4:39). Love moves us to cling to Him for He is our life (Deut. 30:20). Augustine said, "Thou hast made us for Thyself, and our heart is restless until it rests in Thee."

Love God with all that you are. Some people view love only as a good feeling someone gives you. Others think that love is a mere choice of the will, gutting it of affection. Scripture makes it clear that love cannot be limited to a particular part of man, but must rule all of man's inner life and outer activity: "with all thine heart, and with all thy soul, and with all thy strength." The "heart" and "soul" refer to thoughts, emotions, motives, and will. The term "strength" means force or energy. To love God is to keep His commandments (Deut. 5:10; 7:9).

Love starts in the heart and mind but leads to action; it makes us like Josiah, eager and busy serving God (2 Kings 23:25). Wilhelmus à Brakel writes, "Love is the sweet motion of the heart toward God—infused into the hearts of believers by the Holy Spirit—whereby they, by virtue of union with Him and in view of His perfections, delight themselves in God, and in a joyous embrace of His will, fully surrender themselves to His service."

The key word of the commandment is "all." God requires nothing less than the complete devotion to Him of every motion of your body and soul. It is not enough to put God on your list, or even to make Him the top priority on your list. God must own the list, and be written on every line. Augustine wrote, "He loves Thee too little, who loves anything together with Thee, which he loves not for Thy sake."

How humbling is this law! Calvin said, "The perfection which is here required shows with sufficient clearness how far we are from a thorough obedience to the law." We love ourselves, but the best of Christians loves God imperfectly, and the wicked hate Him.

How can we love God with all our hearts?

First, grasp hold of the gospel of "the LORD thy God" (Deut. 6:5). Do not try to love an absolute God, considered merely as a Creator and Lawgiver. Love Him as the God of the covenant, the God of salvation. His love shines supremely in the death of Christ for our sins (Rom. 5:8), and our love is but a Spirit-worked response to His glorious grace (1 John 4:9–10, 13, 19). The law commands love, but only the gospel of Jesus Christ produces love. Brakel says, "Believers on earth love Him, their hearts go out after Him, and He is the focal point of the passions of their love.... All their asking, crying, and weeping is for Jesus."

Second, meditate much on Scripture so that "these words" will be "in thine heart" (Deut. 6:6). Each day repeat to yourself truth you read in the Bible or heard from the preacher of the Word—and preach it to yourself until it stirs your heart to love. Treasure up God's words in your heart as the divine medicine to the lies and seduction of the gods of this world (Deut. 11:16–18).

Third, "teach" the Word to your children in family worship (Deut. 6:7). The term "teach" here has the root meaning of sharpen: we must not let the Word touch the surface of our family's life but penetrate through pointed application. Read the Bible with your family each day, discuss its meaning and application, and then talk about it all day long.

The best way to love God with all your might is to bring the Word of Christ into all your life through the means of grace being blessed to you by the Holy Spirit.

The Fear of God

There are scores of verses in the Bible calling on us to fear God and instructing us what this fear of God is (for example, Deut. 31:12; Pss. 33:8; 111:10; Prov. 23:17). This is true in both Testaments; there is no warrant to think the fear of God is an Old Testament idea, no longer applicable (for example, Matt. 10:28; Luke 1:50; Phil. 2:12; Rev. 19:5). Essentially, to fear God means to reverence, love, trust, and live for God alone. It's the whole of true religion (Eccl. 12:13). John Brown of Haddington captured the fear of God in these words: "The happiness of Christians is in the love of God, and the light of his countenance is their life. It matters little to them that the world frowns on them, if he smiles; and it matters little to them that the world smiles, if he frowns."

We were created in such a way that we had the proper fear of God in our hearts. In our fall, however, we sought to cast off that fear of God, though there are remnants of it in our consciences. Many fallen sinners still have a certain dread and apprehension of God, especially when they find God coming against them in temporal judgments. None of this of itself is saving, however. Romans 3:18 makes clear that by nature there is no true fear of God before our eyes. The fear of the Lord is a gift of God from His gracious covenant (Jer. 32:39–40). The Holy Spirit works in the hearts of sinners to instill the fear of God, bring it into exercise, and nurture it (Ps. 86:11). This fear of the Lord is "clean, enduring forever" (Ps. 19:9).

Do you know this fear of God? To truly fear God, first, means you respect and reverence Him as the holy God (Isa. 8:15). God is God and we are not. This should be ample reason for the true fear of Him. Also, He has revealed Himself both in creation and in His Word as all-wise, all-powerful, holy, just, and good. He ought to be held in utmost reverence because of who He is and how He has revealed Himself. Every blade of grass is a call for us to fear God. Every breath we breathe increases our responsibility to fear Him rightly.

To truly fear God, secondly, means you will worship Him as He has instructed us to do (Pss. 5:7; 89:7; Heb. 12:28). We should not pretend that we know of ourselves how to fear Him. He has not, however, left us in the dark as to how to do that. The Bible instructs us clearly and precisely how to approach Him.

To truly fear God, thirdly, means you will hate and flee from sin. Proverbs 8:13 explains: "The fear of the Lord is to hate evil: pride, and arrogancy, and the evil way, and the froward mouth, do I hate."

To truly fear God, fourthly, means you will live out of the forgiveness of sins opened up in the gospel of Christ. Psalm 130:4 says, "But there is forgiveness with thee, that thou mayest be feared." This is not a single experience; as Paul instructs, it involves seeking cleansing again and again. "Having therefore these promises, dearly beloved, let us cleanse ourselves from all filthiness of the flesh and spirit, perfecting holiness in the fear of God" (2 Cor. 7:1).

To truly fear God, fifthly, means you are spoiled and ruined for this world, as Noah was. We read that Noah, "moved with fear, prepared an ark to the saving of his house; by the which he condemned the world, and became heir of the righteousness which is by faith" (Heb. 11:7).

To truly fear God, sixthly, means you will long to commune with others who fear Him (Mal. 3:16). Additionally, you want to see the fear of God spread to the coming generations and throughout the world (Ps. 34:11; Josh. 4:24).

To truly fear God, lastly, means you always desire to know God better. The fear of the Lord is the beginning of wisdom (Prov. 9:10). But when we fear God rightly we will never feel we have enough of that knowledge (Prov. 2:5).

Living by the Ten Commandments

Are the Ten Commandments still relevant for the life of the Christian? Obviously there is considerable discussion about this very point in Christian circles. We remember however that Christ said He did not come to abolish the law but to fulfill it (Matt. 5:17), and He said that with the moral law exemplified in the Ten Commandments especially in mind (Matt. 5:21, 27). The better we understand the law the more we will love and serve our Savior. The Ten Commandments teach us something of Christ (Luke 24:27).

First, for Christians, the Ten Commandments reveal the extent of Christ's atonement for us. The Bible teaches that the Lord Jesus died for our sins (1 Cor. 15:3). If we neglect God's law, we might think that we do not have many sins at all, falsely believing then that Christ's death was not really that necessary. However, when we realize the full implications of the law (Matt. 5:17-48), we then understand more clearly what Christ endured for us on the cross (Rom. 3:20, 25). Christ died for all our sins, suffering the full penalty that our guilt deserved. Therefore, the more clearly we understand the Ten Commandments, the more grateful we will truly be to God for our deliverance through Christ's death.

Second, the more we understand God's law, the more clearly we view the full extent of Christ's perfect obedience. The Bible assures us that although the Lord Jesus was "made under the law" (Gal. 4:4), He "fulfilled all righteousness" (Matt. 3:15), and "did no sin" (1 Peter 2:22). As you consider the Ten

Commandments in their perfection, consider Christ as the perfect Law-keeper. He is the One who lived in perfect obedience to God's holy law. Every action of our Lord Jesus was perfect in accordance with that law: no thought our Lord Jesus had ever contradicted the law of God; every word He spoke was the perfect word of God. Such was the perfection of Christ.

Third, the law teaches us the perfect righteousness that is imputed to us (Rom. 5:18-19). If we are joined to Him by saving faith, then God regards us as if we kept the whole law. Thus the law of God shows us the perfect righteousness we have in Christ. Upon our faith in the Lord Jesus, our transgressions of the law are laid upon Him—and He atones for those sins by His suffering and death. But also by faith in Him, His perfect obedience of the law is imputed to us—so perfectly that God looks upon us as cloaked in the perfection of Christ! The Heidelberg Catechism says it beautifully in answering, "How art thou righteous before God?" by stating: "God, without any merit of mine, but only out of mere grace, grants and imputes to me, the perfect satisfaction, righteousness and holiness of Christ; even so, as if I never had had, nor committed any sin: yea, as if I had fully accomplished all that obedience which Christ has accomplished for me" (Q. 60).

Fourth, the law teaches us the moral beauty of Christ being formed in us—the goal towards which Christians must strive in their sanctification. Paul teaches us that the Ten Commandments illuminate what love means, and are fulfilled when we truly love each other (Rom. 13:8-10). Then, just a few verses later, he writes, "But put ye on the Lord Jesus Christ, and make not provision for the flesh, to fulfil the lusts thereof." Therefore, we put on Christ more and more when, looking to Him by faith, we obey God's law and grow more like Him.

When you hear the Ten Commandments, think of the Lord Jesus Christ. Think of your transgressions of the law and how Christ atoned for them. That will give you a grateful heart towards Him! Think of the perfection of Christ as He lived perfectly in accordance with the Ten Commandments and imputed His righteousness to you by faith. And consider the practical holiness that Christ works in you as He dwells in your heart by the Holy Spirit. This will make you realize that Christ is your all in all!

Godly Contentment

Paul writes in Philippians 4:11b, "I have learned, in whatsoever state I am, therewith to be content." Is this not the Christian's distinct calling and wonderful privilege, that is, to have and to demonstrate true contentment in life? See, for example, Hebrews 13:5, 1 Timothy 6:6, Philippians 4:6–7, and Psalm 37:4. Do you know and glow with Christian contentment in life?

Christian contentment is not only "an embracing of the providence of God," as one put it, but even more fundamentally, an embracing of the God of providence. Wilhelmus à Brakel states in his helpful chapter on this subject that contentment "is not a mental determination to keep ourselves satisfied, but a disposition of the soul . . . . The stronger faith is, the greater the contentment with the will of God will also be." Contentment is not to be found in having favorable circumstances and many possessions, but it is found in the triune God alone, by living in union and communion with Christ and in obedience and service before the Lord (Ps. 23).

The lie of Satan as told in Genesis 3 and replayed in history ever since is that contentment can be found apart from God. Have you seen through this deception of the devil for yourself? This ungodly world is experiencing the miseries of countless forms of discontentment and fading dreams, living in rebellion and unbelief before God (Isa. 57:20–21). Confessing Christians should shine forth the gracious fruit of peaceful contentment in our restless world of rampant murmurings (Phil. 2:14–15). Do you let your light shine with the grace of contentment even in dark and difficult circumstances?

Christian contentment is learned as we genuinely and constantly look to Christ, the Savior of sinners, in Spirit-worked repentance and faith, and so discover what a graciously complete and completely gracious Savior Jesus is (Col. 2:9–10). As Brakel put it, "If you have the all-sufficient One as your salvation, are you then still in need of anything else? Is He not better to you than a thousand worlds? . . . Therefore, speak and practice what the godly did. 'The Lord is my portion, saith my soul; therefore will I hope in Him' (Lam. 3:24)."

Jeremiah Burroughs wrote similarly in his classic, *The Rare Jewel of Christian Contentment*: "A Christian finds satisfaction in every circumstance by getting strength from another, by going out of himself to Jesus Christ, by his faith acting upon Christ and bringing the strength of Jesus Christ into his own soul, he is thereby enabled to bear whatever God lays on him, by the strength that he finds from Jesus Christ."

Do you affirm and demonstrate that while looking to Christ and abiding in Him and His Word under the ministry of the Holy Spirit there is no reason for any discontentment whatsoever, but only for true and growing contentment? The Good Shepherd calls His people to confess "my cup runneth over" (Ps. 23:5) in praise and honor to our triune God and in anticipation of heaven to come. Are you demonstrating this holy, happy contentment at home, school, church, and work? What areas in your life can you grow in by having and showing Christian contentment?

To move us from discontentment to contentment, the Savior calls to us, "Open thy mouth wide, and I will fill it.... He should have fed them also with the finest of the wheat: and with honey out of the rock should I have satisfied thee" (Ps. 81:10b, 16).

Praise God who will lead His people in endless and everlasting contentment! All honor to Him, our Savior God, from whom all blessings flow—including real contentment! Consider what Paul says in 1 Timothy 6:6: "But godliness with contentment is great gain." Are you enrolled in the school of Christ for the gift and prize of Christian contentment? The "God of all comfort" (2 Cor. 1:3) still welcomes more students, in and through Jesus Christ. "For ye know the grace of our Lord Jesus Christ, that though he was rich, yet for your sakes he became poor, that ye through his poverty might be rich" (2 Cor. 8:9).

Self-Denial

Self-denial is one of the defining elements of the followers of Christ. The Lord Jesus states in Luke 9:23, "If any man will come after me, let him deny himself, and take up his cross daily, and follow me." Self-denial is an absolute requirement: if there is no self-denial, there is no following Christ. Since self-denial is so important, it is vital we know what it really is and how to do it.

What is Christian self-denial? Christ demands denying anything in our lives that opposes full faith in and obedience to His Word. As Thomas Watson points out, there are times when a Christian must deny his appetites, his ease, his finances, even his life. Yet what is the core of self-denial? The great Scottish preachers Ebenezer Erskine and James Fisher give a simple and accurate description of self-denial in their Assembly's Shorter Catechism Explained. They describe self-denial as giving up three things in particular.

The first thing to be given up is self-wisdom. We give up self-wisdom "when we are made to see our own depraved reason to be but folly, when compared with the wisdom of God revealed in his word (1 Cor. 3:19)."

The second thing to be given up is self-will. Self-will is given up "when God's will of precept becomes the sole rule of our heart and life (Ps. 119:105) and His will of providence is cheerfully acquiesced in as the best for us (Rom. 8:28)."

The third thing to be given up is self-righteousness. In giving up self-righteousness, "we submit to the righteousness of God, or found our plea for eternal life wholly and entirely upon the meritorious obedience and satisfaction of Christ, as our surety, in our room and stead (Phil. 3:8–9)."

How do we practice self-denial? Three truths are helpful to remember as we strive by God's grace to deny ourselves, giving up self-wisdom, self-will, and self-righteousness.

First, we find help when we remember we only deny ourselves by the Spirit's power. By His regenerating power, the Spirit shows us the foolishness of our own wisdom and lack of righteousness (Rom. 8:7; 2 Cor. 5:17; Col. 3:10). He reveals our wisdom to be in the person and work of Christ Jesus (Job 33; 1 Cor. 1:24; Heb. 1:1–3). He works in us the desire to deny ourselves (Phil. 2:13) and applies the righteousness of Christ to us (Rom. 3:21–26; Gal. 5:5). When we are tempted to despair at our failure to deny ourselves, we have the sure strength of the Spirit of Christ to encourage us.

Second, we find help in prayer. Prayer demands we give up self-wisdom, self-will, and self-righteousness. Praying to "our Father which art in heaven," confessing His name to be "hallowed," and asking Him to "lead us not into temptation, but deliver us from evil" requires that we set aside our wisdom and trust His. Further, there is no room for self-will when we ask "thy will be done on earth as it is in heaven," and when we confess "thine is the kingdom, and the power, and the glory forever." Lastly, it is impossible to be self-righteous when truly asking "forgive us our debts as we forgive our debtors" (Matt. 6:9–13). When you are struggling with self-denial, particularly with a sin you struggle with habitually, pray; God will answer your prayer and you will be strengthened by His wisdom, His will, and His righteousness.

Third, if we would deny ourselves, we must focus on Christ. It is hard to do any difficult task if we forget the reason why we are doing it. The same principle is true for self-denial. We will have no strength if we are not "looking unto Jesus the author and finisher of our faith" (Heb. 12:2). Further, our Lord says in John 15:4, "Abide in me, and I in you. As the branch cannot bear fruit of itself, except it abide in the vine; no more can ye, except ye abide in me," and in John 15:5, "without me ye can do nothing." We must never forget that Jesus calls us to deny ourselves in the context of following Him: "If any man will come after me, let him deny himself" (Luke 9:23).

Humility

I had a college friend who would occasionally say, tongue-in-cheek, "I am the most humble person I know." Though we knew that he wasn't serious when he said it, it shows how elusive true humility is, for we can so easily become proud of our humility. Yet humility is not optional for the Christian. The Lord Jesus said, "Blessed are the poor in spirit: for theirs is the kingdom of heaven" (Matt. 5:3). He warned, "Except ye be converted, and become as little children, ye shall not enter into the kingdom of heaven" (Matt. 18:3). The Puritan Richard Baxter wrote, "Humility is not a mere ornament of a Christian, but an essential part of the new creature. It is a contradiction in terms to be a Christian, and not be humble."

What is humility? A humble person knows his place before God, willingly carries out his calling toward others, and has an accurate estimate of himself. Humility is embracing our proper place before God. In 1 Peter 5:6, we see that we must humble ourselves before the mighty hand of God. The same truth is communicated in Mark 10:35–45, where the disciples were striving for greatness before God and Christ gives a much-needed lesson in humility. At the beginning of his *Institutes of the Christian Religion*, John Calvin wrote, "Indeed, our very poverty better discloses the infinitude of benefits reposing in God. The miserable ruin, into which the rebellion of the first man cast us, especially compels us to look upward. Thus, not only will we, in fasting and hungering, seek thence what we lack; but, in being aroused by fear, we shall learn humility." Later, Calvin heartily affirms the words of Augustine: "If you ask me concerning the precepts of the Christian religion, first, second, third, and always I would answer, 'Humility.'"

Humility is also dealing faithfully with and carrying out our calling well toward others. Christ establishes this in Matthew 22:39 with His declaration of the second great commandment, "Thou shalt love thy neighbor as thyself." The humble person will do what he can for the greater good of others; he will put forth his best efforts to benefit those around him. Jesus displays the perfect example of humility in the act of washing the feet of His disciples in John 13. He took the form of a servant in order to humble Himself and save others (Phil. 2:7–8). When we obediently do what we are called to do with satisfaction, joy, and purpose we are displaying Christ-like humility. A. W. Tozer said, "It is doubtful whether God can bless a man greatly until He has hurt him deeply"—and we could change the word "hurt" to "humbled." C. H. Spurgeon summarized the first two aspects of humility when he wrote, "Humility makes us ready to be blessed by the God of all grace, and fits us to deal efficiently with our fellow-men."

Lastly, humility is accurately knowing ourselves. This is brought out in Romans 12:3, "For I say, through the grace given me, to every man that is among you, not to think of himself more highly than he ought to think." Calvin often emphasized the link between humility and self-knowledge. Without humility, self-knowledge serves pride but with humility self-knowledge is most blessed. Humility smites our hearts in the awareness of our misery and lack. It also submits to God's word of grace and salvation in His Son (Isa. 66:2). Finally, humility thrives in those disciplined by the Spirit to embark on this life of suffering and vale of tears in the anticipation of heavenly glory.

Here are some helps for humility:

1. Hear—recover a sense of the glory and majesty of hearing God's Word preached or read. The hearing and reading of God's Word is the chief way God works humility and we manifest it.

2. Gather—humility enriches fellowship and fellowship encourages humility. Too often the company we keep fuels our pride; gathering with those who are lonely or in distress can teach us humility.

3. Suffer—submit to God's hand in sickness, afflictions, trials, and persecution. Do not seek the removal of these things until you have learned well your weakness and leaned hard on God's strength.

How We Kill Pride

One can hardly imagine a more difficult activity than to kill pride, particularly in ourselves. This is so, not because there is any lack of it in us, but because pride blinds us to its own existence. Pride blinds us to pride.

Pride is the wellspring of all other sins. It was the first sin that begat all other. Its prevalence is so endemic to the human condition, that it is easy to become desensitized to its presence. But it exists every time we do or think or say anything contrary to God's Word or omit anything expected of us by the living God. How so? Because whenever we sin in any way, whether by omission or commission, we in effect exalt our will above God's. This is pride. Every sin is a manifestation of pride.

Though pride is common, it is an abomination. Pride in the heart is sin (Prov. 21:4). God hates pride (Prov. 6:17; 8:13). He will surely punish the proud (Prov. 15:25; 16:5). The day of the Lord is against all the proud, for the Lord alone will be exalted (Isa. 2:11-12).

How do we kill this beast in others? We do it with patience, compassion, and love. Patience because we ourselves are full of it. Compassion because we know how hateful this sin is to God and how dreadful a person's condition before Him is when caught in pride's clutches. Love because we want to see the other person conformed to God's image, which is the very opposite of pride.

How do we kill pride in ourselves? By several means.

First, we need to frequently consider the cross of Jesus Christ. Why? Because that is the best place to see the true and wretched value of that which opposes God's will. The spiritually and physically pummeled Savior died there because of our pride. A fresh, believing sight of Jesus Christ and Him crucified is a truly divine medicine against pride.

Second, we need the help of others. Having considered the blinding tendency of pride, we note that God often uses others to point out pride in us. We kill our pride by listening to their rebukes. The problem here, of course, is that our pride makes us resistant to receiving hearty counsel from others. And few of us have friends who love us enough to speak the truth in love when we need to hear it. So prayer is needed, in the moment, for the grace and humility to accept what others see, even if we don't see it ourselves.

Third, we need the help of God. It is hard to maintain pride when spending considerable time with the Almighty. Prayerlessness stokes pride; prayer has a quenching tendency.

Fourth, we need to give sober thought to the warnings of Scripture that pride brings horrible consequences. Consider these statements:

"When pride cometh, then cometh shame: but with the lowly is wisdom" (Prov. 11:2).

"Pride goeth before destruction, and an haughty spirit before a fall. Better it is to be of an humble spirit with the lowly, than to divide the spoil with the proud" (Prov. 16:18-19).

"A man's pride shall bring him low: but honour shall uphold the humble in spirit" (Prov. 29:23).

Our pride not only hurts us but also harms others. Pride makes us arrogant mockers towards other people (Prov. 21:24). The proud person stirs up fights and conflicts (Prov. 13:10; 28:25).

Finally, let us consider well Paul's reminder to the Corinthians, "Who maketh thee to differ from another? and what hast thou that thou didst not receive? now if thou didst receive it, why dost thou glory, as if thou hadst not received it?" (1 Cor. 4:7-8). Whatever our abilities, our attainments, our acquisitions—all are gifts. Paul's motto should be our practice: "God forbid that I should glory, save in the cross of our Lord Jesus Christ, by whom the world is crucified unto me, and I unto the world" (Gal. 6:14).

We must have no tolerance for pride. We do not correct a venomous snake; we behead it. Pride, like a fire revived, needs to be stamped out lest we be consumed in the conflagration. Hasten the day, Lord, when pride will be extinguished once and forever!

Coping with Criticism

No one likes criticism. Christians with sensitive consciences may find criticism even more difficult to handle. Here are nine ways to help you cope with it.

First, consider criticism inevitable. If you're living as a Christian in a hostile world that hates what you believe, you can't escape criticism. Jesus said that the world will hate us even as it hated Him (John 15:18; 1 John 3:1). He added in Luke 6:26, "Woe unto you, when all men shall speak well of you."

Second, consider the source. Though you should take every criticism seriously, it is still wise to ask yourself: who is criticizing me? Is my critic a friend or a foe, a mature believer or a hardened unbeliever, a highly critical individual, or perhaps a fringe member of the church? If your critic is someone known for wisdom, you should encourage his or her constructive evaluation.

Third, consider timing and prayer. The physical setting, timing, and situation out of which criticism comes may help you determine whether the criticism is helpful. As a general rule, don't respond to criticism for at least twenty-four hours to allow yourself time to pray, think, and get counsel.

Fourth, consider yourself. The Holy Spirit uses our critics to keep us from exalting ourselves. So let yourself be vulnerable. Don't be afraid to say, "I was wrong; will you forgive me?" Be grateful that you can learn valuable truths from your critics. Some of our best friends are those who disagree with us lovingly, openly, and intelligently. "Faithful are the wounds of a friend" (Prov. 27:6).

Fifth, consider the content. Ask yourself honestly: What are my critics saying that might help me improve myself? Is there a kernel of truth in this particular criticism that, if changes are made, will make me more godly? If critics say something constructive, absorb it, confess your fault, take the lead in self-criticism, ask for forgiveness wholeheartedly, make changes for the better, and move on. If the critics offer nothing constructive, be kind and polite, and move on. Either way, move on—don't harbor internal bitterness. Fight God's battles, not your own, and you will discover that He will fight yours (Rom. 12:19).

Sixth, consider Scripture. Memorize and meditate upon texts such as Ephesians 6:10, "Be strong in the Lord, and in the power of his might," as well as Romans 12:10: "Be kindly affectioned one to another with brotherly love." When critics attack and you can't understand God's ways, trust Jesus' words in John 13:7, "What I do thou knowest not now; but thou shalt know hereafter."

Seventh, consider Christ. Above all, look to Jesus in the face of mounting criticism. Hebrews 12:3 advises, "Consider him that endured such contradiction of sinners against himself." Peter is more detailed: "Christ also suffered for us, leaving us an example, that ye should follow his steps: who did no sin, neither was guile found in his mouth; who, when he was reviled, reviled not again; when he suffered, he threatened not; but committed himself to him that judgeth righteously" (1 Peter 2:21–23).

Eighth, consider love. Love your critic. Seek to understand him. Thank him for coming directly to you with his criticism. Be willing to forgive any injury done to you. Pray for your critic, and if possible, pray with your critic— with integrity and humility. Put away anything that inhibits love. As Peter writes, "Laying aside all malice, and all guile, and hypocrisies, and envies, and all evil speakings" (1 Peter 2:1). When you do this, you will discover that your own wounds will heal more rapidly.

Ninth, consider eternity. Remember, all criticism for us as true believers is temporary. Our faithful Savior will be waiting for us on the other side of Jordan. He will wipe away every tear from our eye and will prove to be the Friend who sticks closer than a brother. All wrongs will be made right. There our believing critics will embrace us, and we them. We will understand that all the criticism we received here below was used in the hands of our Potter to prepare us for Immanuel's land. We will see fully that all criticisms were but a light affliction compared to the weight of glory that awaited us.

Enduring Affliction

The psalmist says, "Many are the afflictions of the righteous: but the Lord delivereth him out of them all" (Ps. 34:19). God does not distinguish His people from unbelievers by exempting them from affliction. He distinguishes them by causing all things—even their afflictions—to work out for their spiritual good and eternal deliverance (Rom. 8:28). But how should we respond to afflictions in order to best assure that we properly submit to Him in times of affliction? Think of not only persecution, but also grief, an accident, physical sickness, depression, unemployment, a strained family relationship, abuse, or any other hardship. Any of these can trouble our souls and we might ask, "Why?"

God has His sovereign purpose for everything. Whatever God is doing, it is better for us to ask submissively: "Lord, what must I do? How should I respond so that this works for my good and Thy honor?"

The Bible's answer is not an extensive "how-to" list that taps into man's inner potential, but simply says, "by faith." Faith directs us to entrust ourselves to God. Faith is exercised in a variety of ways, but every proper response to affliction is rooted in faith.

This is best illustrated by Hebrews 11. Hebrew Christians faced all kinds of afflictions in a hostile culture. To encourage them to persevere as Christians, the apostle pointed to Old Testament saints as examples. Here we find a wide spectrum of afflictions. We can only list a few samples:

How could Enoch endure living in such wicked times just before the Flood (Heb. 11:5)? How can you spiritually survive in the wicked culture of our godless society? The same way Enoch did. Faith in God must be a living part of your daily walk. If God is for you, what can man do to you (Rom. 8:31)?

How could Abram leave his homeland, not knowing where the Lord was leading him (Heb. 11:8)? Is God taking you down an unfamiliar path? How can you avoid anxiety? As Abram did: by faith in the Lord who "leads you in the way you should go" (Isa. 48:17).

How could Moses' parents obey God rather than Pharaoh's wicked command (Heb. 11:23)? How can we stand up against the immoral trends of our infant-killing culture and obey God rather than man? Only by faith in the Lord who is the sovereign King of kings.

How could Moses choose to "suffer affliction with God's people" and resist the temptation of Egypt's treasures and pleasures (Heb. 11:25)? The same way Joseph ran from a seductress. By faith in the Lord, whose name they did not forget in Egypt (Gen. 39:9). By faith they valued the "reproach of Christ" more than Egypt's treasures and pleasures and saw "him who is invisible" (Heb. 11:27).

Hebrews 11 also mentions that believers faced other dangers (Heb. 11:27–30). They "stopped the mouth of lions, quenched the violence of fire..." (Heb. 11:33ff). How? These believers had no super powers (James 5:17). It was simply by faith. Not that faith itself is a "magical potion" for physical or even psychological strength. While humanly weak, faith connected their soul to Christ (2 Cor. 12:10). For His Son's sake, God puts all things under Christ's feet for their good (Eph. 1:22). He also renews and sanctifies believers, preparing and preserving them for glory. Faith unites them to the victorious One (1 John 5:4–5). Therefore they can endure "all things through Christ" (Phil. 4:13).

If you are afflicted but still an unbeliever, then you are in great danger. Your temporal affliction is a prelude to eternal affliction. Your affliction calls you to repent and believe. For the believer, affliction is also a call to persevere in faith. Do not stumble in unbelief at your struggle. "Is any among you afflicted? Let him pray" (James 5:13). Call upon the Lord in the day of your trouble (Ps. 50:15). Believer, remember that Christ also "was oppressed and afflicted" (Isa. 53:7). Continue "looking unto Jesus the author and finisher of our faith; who for the joy that was set before him endured the cross" (Heb. 12:2). The best way to cope with affliction is by faith in Christ, who exchanged His cross for a crown.

Spiritual Desertion

The opening verse of Psalm 130, "Out of the depths have I cried to Thee, O God," vividly portrays the gut-wrenching cry emanating from a soul deep-stricken with a loss of its sense of God's presence. John Owen confessed to a young man who was seeking counsel from him that for twenty years he had preached of the one Mediator between God and man without possessing experiential knowledge of what he was proclaiming—until, as he says, "I was brought to the mouth of the grave, and under which my soul was oppressed with horror and darkness."

This is the soul malady known as spiritual desertion and is a cross known only to the child of God. It refers to the depths into which our sovereign God at times, and according to His good pleasure, allows His people to plunge headlong (Ps. 88). However profound these depths may be, they are not the depths of hell draped with the mist of darkness; there is in them no malice, condemnation, or wrath. Sink as the regenerate soul may into unfathomable depths of dread darkness, it ever finds the Rock of Ages beneath. The unregenerate indeed know of these depths but not in the manner of God's children. It brings them no nearer to God and even serves to drive them further from God (Rev. 16:9).

The question, however, that arises deep within the heart of every believer is, "Why have I fallen into this God-forsaken pit? Has God finally rejected me and turned His face?" There is an acute loss of the sense of God's love in which the soul had previously delighted (Rom. 8:15; 1 Peter 1:8). But rest assured it is God who, in His fatherly way, sends and governs these abandonments.

The most common cause for this soul distress arises from the existence, power, and ever-deceiving remnants of indwelling sin in the regenerate. The believer may and must have the abiding assurance that once the Holy Spirit renews the soul in the cleansing from sin, he is a new creature in Christ. But the same Holy Spirit never uproots the principle and root of sin from his heart; it will remain as a plague to the end (Rom. 7:24). We stand painfully amazed as the plough of the Spirit tears through new areas of corruption within the heart, revealing once more the depths of corruption contained there. You who have fled to Christ for refuge, never imagine that your warfare is over.

Then there are also those outbreaks of sin appearing as the fruit of sin's baneful presence within, bringing with them the grievous consequence of conscious loss of communion with God. This can be the experience of even the most mature believer (Ps. 51). Who can fully describe the depth of sorrow occasioned by the awareness of willful departure from the Lord, such as Peter when he went out and "wept bitterly"?

Times of perceived spiritual desertion also come upon those who are plunged into mental affliction. Many gracious souls have been immersed in the dread night of depression where no light is visible on any side. Octavius Winslow wrote, "Through many a dark, starless night the spiritual voyager ploughs the ocean to the desired haven where he would be." And then, because mind and body are so intimately connected, so too the onset of debilitating physical illness can bring an intense season of night upon the soul.

Yet if ever there is a place where the gentleness and sympathy of Christ is abundantly present, it is beside the one who is suffering mental torment and intense physical affliction (Isa. 42:3). With great patience and concern, He draws near to His own who have been plunged into the dark hole of melancholy. He remembers that we are but dust, and from no heart in the entire universe does such loving compassion, tenderness, and sympathy flow as that from the heart of Christ (Ps. 103:13–14).

Isaiah 50:10 gives this counsel, "Who is among you that feareth the Lord, that obeyeth the voice of his servant, that walketh in darkness, and hath no light? Let him trust in the name of the Lord, and stay upon his God." In the darkness, walk by faith and not by sight.

Fleeing Worldliness

Worldliness is when I absorb and embrace a way of thinking and living that is not submissive to God but is instead contrary to God. Worldliness is what the apostle John calls "the lust of the flesh, and the lust of the eyes, and the pride of life" (1 John 2:16). In our experiences in life, we are always meeting worldly thinking and worldly influence and worldly pressure. This worldliness aims to access our own souls and, sadly, too often gets in.

The Bible teaches us to flee worldliness. To flee means to run away as far as possible and fast as possible. John writes to Christians, "Love not the world" (1 John 2:15). Paul urges in Romans 12:2, "Be not conformed to this world." What both mean is that we are to live in such a way that we reject all sinful ways of thinking and living influenced by the devil. That is to flee worldliness.

So how do we do that?

In the first place, let us seek to be renewed in our minds. Paul writes in Romans 12:2, "And be not conformed to this world; but be ye transformed by the renewing of your mind." If we are not going to be conformed to this world but truly transformed, then we have to experience mind renewal through exposure to and absorption of God's Word, all blessed to us by the Holy Spirit. If we would flee worldliness, how diligent we should be in careful and prayerful reading and hearing of Scripture.

Already this point can be a test for us. If we are not getting new minds, very likely we are very worldly. Let us start with this basic, most fundamental point: "by the renewing of your mind." So open the Bible. Read it with attention and prayer. Listen to it preached. Think over it constantly and discuss it with others. That's the start.

In the second place, to flee worldliness, let us commit to doing God's will. John writes about this in 1 John 2. He makes the key point in verse 17 that "the world passeth away, and the lust thereof." And then John says, "he that doeth the will of God abideth for ever." John is contrasting those who love the world with those who do not love it. Those who do not love it are those who do God's will. It is both a mark of the godly and the way to godliness. When we engage in joyful, thankful obedience to the Lord, then we find the world has no power over us. This too is a test. Do you aim to do God's commandments? Won't this help you to flee worldliness?

There is a third point to consider. John talks about the love of the Father. He writes in 1 John 2:15, "Love not the world, neither the things that are in the world. If any man love the world, the love of the Father is not in him." If you love the world, you don't love the Father. And that means that you don't know His love and you don't show Him love. But if you know the Father's love shed abroad in your heart through the Holy Spirit, and also show Him love, how can you love the world? To use the form of the text but changing the words, "If any man love the Father, the love of the world is not in him." It just can't be!

So this too is a test. Maybe it's the ultimate test. You cannot flee worldliness unless you love the Father. But then, how can Christians not love the Father? Is He not "the Father of mercies and God of all comfort" (2 Cor. 1:3), especially through His own beloved Son, Jesus Christ? And is He not all this even to undeserving sinners like us? Therefore, let us not love the world. What can it do for us? And besides, it is passing away (1 John 2:17). Let us not love the world, but let us love the all-beautiful Father, together with His all-glorious Son, and the ever-blessed Holy Spirit. Let us love the triune God—really love Him, by the Spirit's grace. That is the way to flee worldliness.

Fighting against Backsliding

Backsliding is a season of increasing sin and decreasing obedience in those who profess to be Christians. Not every sin is backsliding. Christians must sadly expect their lives to consist of a continual cycle of sinning and repenting of sin by faith in Christ crucified (1 John 1:9—2:2). In backsliding, however, this cycle of repentance is largely broken and spiritual ground is lost. The longer we persist in backsliding, the less right we have to claim to be true Christians (1 John 2:3-4), for repentance is of the essence of true Christianity (Acts 2:38; 20:21).

Backsliding from Christ is thus a serious matter. It dishonors God, disregards Christ as Savior, grieves the Spirit, tramples God's law underfoot, and abuses the gospel. And it is a sin as common as it is terrible. God laments in Hosea 11:7 that His people are "bent"—that is, prone— to backslide from Him. The propensity to sin resides in all of our hearts, as does a deep desire to avoid repentance. Little wonder, then, that God warns us so often in Hosea, Jeremiah, and other prophets to abhor and fight against backsliding.

Backsliding usually begins when believers let themselves drift from God, His Word, and His ways. We then slip away gradually, sometimes imperceptibly. One weakness leads to another. Most commonly, backsliding begins with coldness in prayer and then moves to indifference under the Word. Inner corruptions then multiply. The world is loved more and fellow believers are loved less. Man-centered hopes soon replace God-centered desires.

Backsliding reaps bitter results. It injures God's holy and worthy name. It makes us spiritually numb so that our consciences become desensitized, and it results in the church's overall decay.

So how do we fight against this abominable sin—a sin that is so unworthy of our Lord?

First, we must return to the Lord and stop running from Him. We must heed Hosea 14:1, "Return unto the Lord thy God, for thou hast fallen by thine iniquity." We must repent by recognizing our sinful condition, remembering our past obedience, searching out our sin, grieving over it, confessing it, and fleeing from it.

Second, we must pursue righteousness by returning to Christ Jesus. To that end, we must return to a diligent use of the means of grace. That means returning seriously to the Bible. Attend diligently to sound preaching of it. Read it privately every day. Share regular devotions in your family. Memorize and meditate on key verses. Engage in a serious Bible study with one or more friends.

It also means returning diligently to prayer, even when you do not feel like it. Hosea 14:2 says: "Take with you words and turn to the Lord: say unto him, Take away all iniquity, and receive us graciously." Pray the Scriptures back to God. Attend and pray at prayer meetings. Pray with close friends. Pray daily in and with your family. Pray for the Holy Spirit to restore the weeks, months, or perhaps even years, that the locusts have eaten (Joel 2:25).

Read solid, sound Christian literature that will do your soul good. As you read, pray much for grace—justifying grace, sanctifying grace, adopting grace, reviving grace, strengthening grace, reviving grace, and sovereign grace. Buttress your reading by journaling and/or finding an accountability partner. Two good spiritually minded friends will do you more good than ten or twenty friends who may be Christians but with whom you cannot communicate from heart to heart.

Above all, take refuge to Christ Jesus every day—yes, ten times a day. Flee to Him as your Savior and Lord, your righteousness and strength, your justification and sanctification, your praying and thanking High Priest, and your able and wise Physician. Let Him be your all-in-all.

Don't rest until you are in your old way of communion with Christ again. And be assured, He will receive you back. He is a Savior of second chances; He delights to forgive even seventy times seven.

Come back home to your approachable Savior who loves to receive penitent sinners. Welcome home penitent, backsliding prodigal—welcome home in Christ to the Father's arms, lips, words, and tears of mercy (Luke 15:20-24). Your God and Savior delights in mercy (Micah 7:18). By the Spirit's grace, believe this amazing truth, embrace it, and live it out.

Family Worship

In today's churches, many young people become nominal members with mere notional faith or abandon evangelical truth for unbiblical doctrine and modes of worship. One major reason for this failure is the lack of emphasis upon family worship.

Joshua 24:14–15 says, "Now therefore fear the Lord, and serve him in sincerity and in truth: and put away the gods which your fathers served on the other side of the flood, and in Egypt; and serve ye the Lord. And if it seem evil unto you to serve the Lord, choose you this day whom ye will serve; whether the gods which your fathers served that were on the other side of the flood, or the gods of the Amorites, in whose land ye dwell: but as for me and my house, we will serve the Lord."

Notice three things in this text: first, Joshua did not make worship or service to the living God optional; second, Joshua enforces the service of God in families with his own example; and third, the word serve in verse 15 is an inclusive word, which is translated as worship many times in Scripture. Surely every God-fearing husband, father, and pastor must say with Joshua: "As for me and my household, we will serve the Lord. We will seek the Lord, worship Him, and pray to Him as a family. We will read His Word, replete with instructions, and reinforce its teachings in our family."

Given the importance of family worship as a potent force in winning untold millions to gospel truth throughout the ages, we ought not be surprised that God requires heads of households do all they can to lead their families in worshiping the living God. Our families owe their allegiance to God. God has placed us in a position of authority to guide our children in the way of the Lord (Eph. 6:4). Clothed with holy authority, we owe to our children prophetical teaching, priestly intercession, and royal guidance.

Heads of households, we must implement family worship in the home. God requires that we worship Him not only privately as individuals, but publicly as members of the covenant body and community, and socially as families. Here are some suggestions to help you establish God-honoring family worship in your homes.

According to Scripture, God should be served in special acts of worship in families today in the following three ways:

1. Daily instruction in the Word of God. God should be worshiped by daily reading and instruction from His Word. Have a plan, account for special occasions, involve the family, and encourage private Bible reading and study. Through questions and answers, parents and children are to daily interact with each other about sacred truth (Deut. 6:6–7). For biblical instruction, strive to be plain in meaning, pure in doctrine, relevant in application, and affectionate in manner. Be sure to require attention.

2. Daily prayer to the throne of God. Jeremiah 10:25 says, "Pour out thy fury upon the heathen that know thee not, and upon the families that call not on thy name." As Thomas Brooks said, "A family without prayer is like a house without a roof, open and exposed to all the storms of heaven." For praying, be short, be simple without being shallow, be direct, be natural yet solemn, and strive for variety.

3. Daily singing the praise of God. Psalm 118:15 says, "The voice of rejoicing and salvation is in the tabernacles [or

homes] of the righteous: the right hand of the Lord doeth valiantly." That is a clear reference to singing. The psalmist says this sound is (not simply ought to be) in the tents of the righteous. We advise that you sing doctrinally pure songs, sing Psalms first and foremost without neglecting sound hymns, sing simple songs if you have young children, and sing heartily and with feeling.

Some people object to regular times of family worship. Don't indulge excuses to avoid family worship. Let us remember that God often uses the restoration of family worship to usher in church revival. As goes the home, so goes the church. Family worship is a most decisive factor in how the home goes.

Being a Christ-like Husband

Few men appreciate long articles on how to behave—especially as to how we ought to treat our wives, so here, based on Ephesians 5, are our duties summed up in terms of their pattern and their practice.

Christ is our pattern. Our basic precept for marriage is, "Husbands, love your wives, even as Christ also loved the church" (Eph. 5:25a). Following Christ's pattern of loving His bride, each of us is to love his wife in these ways:

1. Absolutely. Christ gives "Himself" for His bride—His total self (v. 25). He holds nothing back. That is obvious from what He has done (think of Calvary), is doing (think of His constant intercession in heaven), and will do (think of His Second Coming). So we too are called to radical, absolute giving of ourselves to our wives in authentic love.

2. Realistically and purposely. Christ goes on loving the church, despite her spots and wrinkles, so that He can present her perfect to His Father in the Great Day (vv. 26-27). Our love must be both realistic (remembering our wives are sinners just like us) and purposeful (aiming for their holiness).

3. Sacrificially. Christ nourishes and cherishes His bride at His own expense (vv. 28-29). So ought we husbands treat our wives at our own expense with the same care that we treat our bodies. If you get something in your eye, you give it immediate, tender care. Do you treat your wife with that same care when she is hurting?

How should we practice this pattern?

Show great interest in your wife as a person. Care about her. Ask her how her day went and how the kids behaved today. Ask her about her dreams, fears, and frustrations. Learn to listen so that she opens up the more.

Pray for your wife privately and with her. Lay out her needs before God. Be earnest in praying for her spiritual growth, and for relief in physical and emotional difficulties. Let her feel your strength and your tenderness on her behalf at God's throne of grace.

Love your wife lavishly. Love her as she is—faults included. Please her (1 Cor. 7:33). Respect and honor her, and treat her tenderly (1 Peter 3:7). Tell her every day how much you love her. Shower her with affection. Cherish her as God's special gift to you.

Heap praise on her. Tell her how beautiful and wonderful she is in your eyes. Be intimate, specific, creative, and repetitive in your compliments. Compliment her kindness, her smile, her dress, her hair, and a thousand other things. Compliment her with affection in your voice, with love in your eyes, and with arms of embrace. Praise her in the presence of others (Prov. 31:28). Never allow the children to speak disrespectfully about her.

Learn what your wife enjoys. Does she enjoy walking together? Walk with her. Eating out? Take her out. Learn to love what she loves as much as possible. Cultivate shared friendship and interests. The more you find to do in common, usually the better your marriage will be. Provide your wife with biblical, tender, clear servant leadership, not ruthless authoritarianism. Following Christ as your pattern, delight in serving her (Matt. 20:25–26). Be the spiritual leader of your wife and children. Be the father-shepherd, a gentle giant in the home.

Never forget the differences between men and women; become an expert in knowing and responding to the way your wife is. Never allow any relationship to take priority over your friendship with your wife. Never criticize her over small things; as for big things, do it with great tenderness and love, at the right time, and in the right setting. Never compare your wife unfavorably to other people, or criticize her in front of other people. Never fail to give your wife sufficient freedom so that she can strive to be her own kind of a Proverbs 31 woman. Do not smother her or try to control her personality. Never stop being a courteous gentleman.

In conclusion, remember this: if both you and your wife put God first, each other second, and yourselves third, you will be guaranteed a truly blessed marriage.

Being a Godly Wife

God's perfect plan for families includes the creation of men and women as well as how they are to relate to one another. We were created perfect; sadly, sin changed that. But God, in His mercy, gave us marriage, a jewel out of Paradise (Gen. 2:18–25). The husband's call to love, nourish, and give himself for his bride, as Christ does for the church, is complemented by the wife's call to respect and submit to him. Together, they are a team. He is the head of the home, providing and protecting (Eph. 5:23). She is at his side, the hub of the wheel in the home. The details vary, but God's plan is timeless. We discard it at our own peril, but when we follow it, we will be blessed.

Zeroing in on the role of a godly wife, the first blessing comes when we submit with contentment to this plan, trusting God's wisdom (Prov. 3:5–6), standing strong against the feminists' drumbeat which says this is degrading, choosing rather to be in God's will, and expecting more blessings.

The godly wife is blessed when she loves God the most of all, and His Word is written on her heart and manifested in her life. She fights the sin that still lives in her by spending time alone with God in prayer and reading (Eph. 6:17–18). Her walk and her talk are light on a hill and salt of the earth. Walking with Him enables her to walk in harmony with her husband.

The godly wife is blessed when she is faithful to her husband. She wholeheartedly gives him her love, affection, commitment, and attention (Titus 2:4). Giving in to temptation is not an option, in spite of his diminishing muscles, increasing girth, gray hair, and their humdrum life. She doesn't look for a new recipe, but spices up the ingredients she has by pouring her energy into her relationship with her husband.

To the single woman who wishes to be a godly wife: pray and choose wisely. Marry a man you are able to respect, not one who is foolish, selfish, angry, or immature. Marry a godly man who loves you for your whole person. Spurgeon advised us to keep our eyes wide open before marriage, and half closed after. So the married woman should focus on her husband's positive characteristics and minimize his irritating idiosyncrasies (Prov. 10:12; 1 Peter 4:8). Isn't that how we wish to be thought of?

Respect your husband (Eph. 5:33). Your respect for your husband begins in your heart and flows out in your tone of voice, facial expressions, affection (or lack of it), and words. He craves your appreciation for his work and acknowledgement of his gifts. Just as he naturally flexes his biceps when you tuck your hand in above his elbow, so he naturally flexes the characteristics you praise.

Enter his world by asking about his day. Keep connected. Discuss the inner thoughts and feelings of your hearts, of natural and spiritual things. Keep romance and intimacy alive. Continue to date. Keep yourself as healthy and attractive as possible. And always be affectionate. Nurture your marriage; it is precious.

The godly wife is also blessed when she submits to her husband (Eph. 5:22, 24). The husband and wife team could be compared to the president and vice-president of a corporation that specializes in servant leadership. They are persons of equal value, as are children and employees, but someone has to be in charge. Husband and wife ought to be best friends who make decisions together for the good of the family. When they can't agree, the husband has the final word (Eph. 5:23).

Some men are difficult to respect and submit to; their wives have the challenging task of rising above their behavior and taking the high road of obeying God (1 Peter 3:1-2). Such a wife is not a doormat, she may not enable or approve sin, but she exercises tough love. She will need to pray for fortitude. She hopes and prays he will be sanctified by her example (1 Cor. 7:10-17).

Blessings will follow the godly wife when she follows God's plan for marriage, and those around her will be blessed as well.

Showing Hospitality

In Genesis 18, Abraham is sitting in his tent and sees three strangers approaching. He runs to meet them, asking them to stay for a meal. He then hurries to prepare food while they wait for him. In the end, Abraham discovers that his guests are the Lord Himself and two angels. Hebrews 13:2 says, "Be not forgetful to entertain strangers: for thereby some have entertained angels unawares." Abraham's actions here, informed by the rest of Scripture, provide a pattern for our own practice of hospitality.

First, Christian hospitality is welcoming strangers into our homes so that we can minister to them, whether unbelievers or believers. Having friends and family into our homes is not hospitality—that is fellowship, which of course should play a major role in our lives as well. But biblically, hospitality is kindness to strangers; that is what the word means, and that is what we see God's people doing throughout the Bible (see Gen. 19:1-3; Josh. 2:4; Ruth 2:8-10; Judges 19:20; Acts 16:15, 34). Abraham did not know who these men were when they sat down. When is the last time you invited someone you had just met or someone you didn't really know into your home? That was the last time you practiced hospitality.

Second, Christian hospitality is sacrificial. Abraham puts more than twenty liters of flour and a whole calf into the meal—valuable commodities in the ancient Near East! Though he was a rich man, this hospitality still cost him something. Hospitality will cost us as well, whether in time, money, effort, or in some other way. Are you willing to trust

God's provision for us to obey His command to practice hospitality?

Third, Christian hospitality is inconvenient. Though it will not likely mean that we have to kill, clean, and cook a cow, hospitality will involve work, which husband, wife, and children should engage in together. It usually involves arranging schedules, planning and making a meal, keeping up conversation, cleaning up, and dying to self as we love others. Hospitality is not convenient, but it is something that God calls us to do. If that is so, we should do it willingly like Abraham, for God loves the cheerful giver. Can we practice hospitality without grumbling (1 Peter 4:9)?

Fourth, Christian hospitality brings blessing. Scripture links obedience with spiritual blessing. This is as true for hospitality as it is for other biblical commands. It blesses those who are ministered to, and it blesses those who are ministering. Hebrews 13:2 encourages us to practice hospitality by reminding us of Abraham's experience; he entertained angels unawares! Calvin comments, "If someone will object that entertaining angels is an unusual occurrence, I have a ready answer, in the fact that we receive not only angels, but Christ himself, when we receive the poor in his name. If we do it to the least of these brethren, we have done it unto him." Do you believe that God will bless your hospitality for eternal good?

Hospitality is not a gift that God gives to just some of His people. It is true that it is a quality highlighted in the character necessary for an elder (1 Tim. 3:2; Titus 1:8). However, it is also a command for every Christian, regardless of giftedness, social status, economic privilege, or attitude. Romans 12:13 says that believers must be "distributing to the necessity of saints; given to hospitality." When done in love to God and love to our neighbor, it is a delight to God and blessed by Him—and will bless the stranger. Practicing hospitality is the best way to develop ability and cultivate a thankful obedience to the Bible's hospitality commands.

If you are a Christian, God has graciously brought you into reconciled fellowship with Himself after welcoming you through the gospel of His only begotten Son. The day is coming when He will welcome you into His heavenly home, although you were a stranger and enemy. How can you show the love of Christ to strangers in your life today?

Raising Children in the Lord

Children are gifts from God (Ps. 127:3–5). The Lord entrusts them to us with the responsibility to care for them and to raise them in His ways. Ephesians 6:4 says, "And, ye fathers, provoke not your children to wrath: but bring them up in the nurture and admonition of the Lord." God gives both father and mother authority over their children (Ex. 20:12; Eph. 6:1–2). They are called to work as a team, with the father as the head of the household (Eph. 5:23), and the wife as his helper in the home (Gen. 2:18; Titus 2:5). They must exercise that authority to love, serve, strengthen, and prepare their children, not to discourage them (Col. 3:21).

Raising children begins before pregnancy, with prayers for future generations (Gen. 25:21). When a baby is conceived, husbands should tenderly care for their wives, and wives for their own bodies, knowing that in so doing they care for a person whom God is forming in the womb (Ps. 139:13–14).

Father and mother should start to labor to bring their children to Jesus, who delights to bless children (Matt. 19:13–15). God has provided powerful means by which parents may raise their children in the Lord. We have already noted praying for your children.

Another means is teaching the Bible to your children. One of the great purposes of the Bible is to equip fathers and mothers to teach their families to hope in the Lord and keep His commandments (Ps. 78:5–7). For this reason, parents must also make sure their children learn to read well, so that they can understand the Bible, catechisms, and other helpful books. A key time for teaching your children in addition to worship with the church is regular family worship in the home (see the article on this topic earlier in this section). However, parents should fill all of life with conversations about God's Word and how it applies (Deut. 6:6–7).

A third means of bringing your children to Jesus is disciplining them in love. Since sin entered into the human race (Rom. 5:12), proud rebellion clings to our hearts, but firm correction will drive it out (Prov. 22:15). The Bible calls this "the rod," referring to spanking. Contrary to popular belief, physical discipline administered to correct disobedience is not an act of abuse or hatred—rather, it is a necessary act of love (Prov. 13:24). By God's grace, the pain of a spanking teaches children lessons about the consequences of sin that can ultimately save their souls (Prov. 23:13–14)— especially when coupled with teaching about God's forgiveness and power in Christ. Failure to discipline one's children will bring shame and grief to parents (Prov. 29:15; 1 Sam. 2:22–36). However, angry parents who discipline in rage only create angry children and a home full of strife (Prov. 15:1, 18; 22:24–25; Eph. 6:4). Wait to discipline until by prayer you can do it with a spirit that is under control (Prov. 16:32). The motive of discipline is love, and its goal is to train a child in righteousness for his own good (Heb. 12:6, 10).

A fourth means of raising your children in the Lord is offering wise counsel. This becomes especially important as your children grow older. They face many difficult decisions about what car to purchase, what vocation to pursue, whom to marry, etc. Parents have valuable experience and insight to share. Even when mom and dad are old, their children should still listen to them (Prov. 23:22). If you have won the respect and friendship of your children over the years, their hearts will be open to hear you (Prov. 23:26).

Lastly, God has given parents the means of living as a godly example. Example is extremely powerful. People who do not practice what they preach only produce more hell-bound hypocrites (Matt. 23:3, 18). However, those who live in sincere godliness can say, "Those things, which ye have both learned, and received, and heard, and seen in me, do: and the God of peace shall be with you" (Phil. 4:9). There is no greater legacy to leave your child than the memories of a father and mother transformed by Christ.

Being a Christian Grandparent

Grandparenting brings both privilege and responsibility. Though Scripture uses the word "grandmother" only once, namely, for Lois, the grandmother of Timothy (2 Tim. 1:5), God does tell us in His Word what He expects from grandparents. Their lives can bless generations to come.

We grandparent already before becoming grandparents. The way we raise our children affects our grandchildren more than anything else we may do. Initially, parents may not look beyond their own children, but God does. The Old Testament is filled with references to "generations to come," "the third and fourth generation," and "children's children." God works through the generations and instructs parents to raise their children in the fear of His name (Ps. 78:1–8).

We grandparent by praising God for grandchildren and praying for them. As prospective grandparents, my wife and I felt a deep sense of wonder regarding the continuity of our family and the presence of the Lord in our lives. We rejoiced that God was crowning the marriages of our children with the gift of children of their own, and grandchildren to us. A deep awareness of the responsibilities of both parents and grandparents and the potential pitfalls drove us to prayer.

It is said of Philip Henry, father of Matthew Henry: "He had, in eight years' time, twenty-four grandchildren; some by each of his children; concerning whom he would often bless God. . . . He thus writes, 'I have now seen my children's children; let me also see peace upon Israel; and then I will say, Lord, now lettest thou thy servant depart.' Some were much affected with it, when he baptized two of his grandchildren together at Chester, publicly, and preached on

Genesis 33:5: 'They are the children which God hath given thy servant.'"

We grandparent by being examples of the fear of God in our lives. My wife and I distinctly remember our own grandparents witnessing their faith through prayer, reading, and singing of psalms, and encouraging and teaching us in turn. Paul speaks in such a way of Timothy's grandmother Lois and his mother Eunice, referring to their "unfeigned faith" (faith without a hint of falsehood). A hypocrite has a basic disconnect between his mouth and his heart, and children are often best at sensing this, even if not articulating it. Lois and Eunice taught Timothy the Scriptures, despite the fact that Timothy's own father remained a Gentile. Knowing the real significance of the Holy Scriptures for your own heart and life, you will wish your children and grandchildren to come under the same Word of God. None of us can open hearts. The Holy Spirit can bring them to the Teacher, who is able to make them wise unto salvation (2 Tim. 3:15).

We grandparent by building relationships with our grandchildren. We need to get to know each grandchild and relate to him at his or her own level. The Bible commands parents to teach their children "along life's way" (Deut. 6:7). We need to gain the trust of each grandchild. Young children enjoy telling and showing us their discoveries, and we can tell them of our own discoveries in the light of God's Word and faithfulness. May the Lord grant that these things may stay with them until they are grandparents themselves and, with His blessing, may be passed along by them to their own grandchildren.

We grandparent by reinforcing the long-range vision of the Scriptures for our grandchildren. There is a wonderful scene in the Bible of Jacob blessing his grandchildren, Ephraim and Manasseh (Gen. 47:9-22). Notice how lovingly Joseph sought the blessing of a godly grandparent over his own children. Jacob expressed this blessing in ways that no doubt left a mark on Ephraim and Manasseh and down through their lines of descent. Grandparents have traversed more hills and valleys of life than parents, and their experience of the Lord's faithfulness can help encourage, challenge, and motivate a longer-range vision.

May the Lord overcome our grandparenting shortcomings and give us grace to grandparent faithfully and fruitfully.

Honoring Your Parents

Imagine as a ten-year-old seeing your three-year-old baby sister trying to open a jar of rat poison. She really wants the "candies" inside! You quickly take the jar out of her hands and put it up on a high shelf out of her reach. She is very upset and cries. She thinks you are really mean for not letting her eat some of the "candy" she found. But you are older and you know better. You know that if she ate the rat poison pellets there would be serious consequences; she would become very sick or maybe even die.

Obeying your parents can be like this at times. Sometimes, as children, your parents tell you that you cannot do something that you really want to do, or they take away something that you want to have. You are upset, and maybe even think that your parents are cruel. But your parents are older and more experienced than you are. They see dangers and potential for harm in what you want to do or to have. Trust and obey your parents. Respect the father and mother that God has given to you. They know you better and love you more than any other adult in the whole world. Obey your parents promptly, willingly, out of a spirit of love and respect; not simply because you must. God sees your heart, your will.

The Fifth Commandment says, "Honour thy father and thy mother, that thy days may be long upon the land which the Lord thy God giveth thee" (Ex. 20:12). Paul likewise wrote, "Children, obey your parents in all things: for this is pleasing unto the Lord" (Col. 3:20).

Obeying and respecting your parents can become even more challenging when you become a teenager. Why? The lines of responsibility between parents and children cross during the teen years. When you were born, your parents did virtually everything for you. They fed you, clothed you, and changed your diapers. Now as you mature into a young adult, you enter a time of transition. You increasingly make more decisions: how to spend your time, where to drive once you have your license, how to deal with a friend who has wronged you, how to spend your money, and whether to apply for a job or not. You increasingly become the decision-maker and your parents step back to let you mature into adulthood.

Two challenges often present themselves during this time of transition.

1. Teens tend to overestimate their own abilities and want too much independency too quickly. Many teens are over-confident because they have not yet experienced very much of life's realities and consequences yet. In other words, teens may want to play with and eat "poison pellets" of temptation and sin because they do not see the dangerous consequences and think confidently, "I know how to take care of myself."

2. Parents tend to resist and give too little independence too slowly to their teen-aged children. This resistance to "let go" arises from parents' deep love and concern for their children's safety and welfare, and their sense of accountability before God. As a teen, how can you help your parents confidently give you more independence and freedom? By building trust. The more your parents trust you, the easier it will be for them to agree to your requests and to grant you more freedom to do things on your own. How can you build trust with your parents?

- Be honest with them, even when you have done wrong.
- Ask for their permission to do things or when a change of plans occurs.
- Show your love for them.
- Communicate with them; readily share with them and be a good listener.
- Try to understand them, thinking about their God-given responsibility and their deep love for you and your welfare.
- Pray for them, even that God would help their weaknesses and faults.
- Trust your parents; willingly respect and obey them.
- Trust that the Lord Jesus can help you to do this; pray much to God for this.

When doing this, by God's grace, you will be blessed as children, as teenagers, all the days of your life on earth, and even eternally! Trust that God's Word and promises are true.

Serving God at Work

The Ten Commandments teach us, "Six days shalt thou labour and do all thy work.... For in six days the Lord made heaven and earth (Ex. 20:9, 11). Our daily work reflects who we are: image-bearers of a God who spends His days working. "The works of the Lord are great," writes the psalmist. They are "honourable... glorious... made... to be remembered" (Ps. 111:3–4). His infinity limits the comparisons between His work and ours. Still, His self-revelation in Scripture shows Him busy with creation, providence, and redemption. God is not passive, simply receiving the praise and accolades that His work deserves; that has its place, but not at the expense of the work He does and expects of His creatures.

The Christian road to work has two ditches. The "work is a necessary evil" ditch contains elements of truth. Work is necessary. "If any would not work, neither should he eat" (2 Thess. 3:10). It also has been warped by the fall. "Cursed is the ground for thy sake," God told Adam in Eden, "in the sweat of thy face shalt thou eat bread" (Gen. 3:17, 19). Thorns and thistles that accompany work are not only physical ones but include the workplace politics, the unjust selfishness that takes advantage of others, and the tedium that is part of every job.

The "worship is more important than work" ditch also is based on truth. To minimize "the necessary evil," some spend as little time as possible working, preferring more spiritual activities. The monastic impulse is expressed not only in historical religious orders but also in current attitudes. Here, work has no spiritual value and is valued only for its completion. Yet there is some truth here. "Seek ye first the kingdom of God, and his righteousness, and all these things shall be added unto you" (Luke 12:33) establishes a clear priority that in our day often is forgotten. Our six days of labor, if not understood in the context of the seventh day of rest in which God is worshipped for His goodness and what He has made, inevitably leads to idolatry.

In these ditches, work is devalued, but the Christian road to work puts it in its God-ordained place. A Christian works in the context of the hopeful groanings of Romans 8. As we carry out our God-given vocations, stewarding the unique gifts He has provided us in the context where His providence has placed us, we experience the "bondage of corruption." But we also recognize that it is through carrying out our calling that we participate in the great story of history which leads from the garden of Genesis 2 to the great city of Revelation 21, in which nations and kings will walk (v. 24). The Christian hope will have physical expression when in our redeemed bodies (Rom. 8:23) we will carry out our vocations perfectly.

Solomon captures something of this "now but not yet" perspective of work, noting that man should "enjoy the good of all his labour, it is the gift of God" (Eccl. 3:13). We receive this gift in a context of life's vanity, recognizing that our calling is to "fear God and keep his commandments" (also the commandment to work) and acknowledging that "God shall bring every work into judgment" (Eccl. 12:13–14).

Those who have been crucified with Christ live in the flesh, Christ living in them (Gal. 2:20). Here is comfort, also for our work. It is Christ's perfect obedience, earned in part in His father's carpenter shop but also in His ministry vocation, that is the evidence that will be considered. Christ's obedience will be judged as being perfect. His blood will cover the penalty for our imperfections, also our workplace sins. And so the Christian goes to work with joy, knowing that He serves and worships a God who also works.

- How does your work utilize the gifts you have been given as an image-bearer of God?

- What are the particular idolatries you are tempted to in your specific work context?

- How does living in the flesh but with Christ in us come to expression in our work?

- How might thinking about the work we will do in the new earth inspire us for our calling today?

Using Leisure Time Well

Most people never have enough leisure time. They view work as a necessary evil to earn enough money to do what they want to do in their free time. They live for their evenings, weekends, and vacations. The recreation and entertainment industries love these people. Then there are others who feel guilty when they are not working. After all, God's Word says we are to "labour" six days and redeem every moment (Ex. 20:9; Eph. 5:16). Where are you in the spectrum between these poles? Neither of these extremes is biblical. Work is not a necessary evil but a God-given calling (Gen. 2:15); leisure time is not from the evil one, but a God-given gift (Eccl. 3:13; 5:18–19; 9:9).

One purpose for leisure time is to be refreshed physically, mentally, and spiritually. That is why God gave us a weekly day of rest, to begin to know Him. While on earth, the Lord Jesus knew He and His disciples needed additional times of rest. After becoming wearied by ministry and receiving the disturbing news of John the Baptist's death, He said to His disciples, "come ye yourselves apart… and rest a while" (Mark 6:31). Times of rest better equip us to work. As the Puritans said, the one who doesn't take time to rest is like the harvester who doesn't pause to sharpen his scythe and ends up being less productive.

Another purpose for leisure time is to strengthen bonds with others. God pronounced His blessing on the God-fearing people who took time to speak "often one to another" (Mal. 3:16). Bonds of family, friends, and church can be strengthened and others blessed in our free time.

Another purpose is the enjoyment of God's gifts (1 Tim. 6:17b). God shows His glory in the wonderful variety and exquisite beauty of His creation. He gives food, marriage, and other things for us to enjoy in thankfulness to Him (1 Tim. 4:4–5).

These purposes ought to govern our activities. Guard against things that conflict with them. Selfishness is one danger. Free time is often considered "my time" in which I am free to do whatever I want (Luke 12:16–21), as if God's call to love Him above all and my neighbor as myself doesn't apply during those hours. So use your free time to benefit others.

Another danger is letting time-wasters consume time without profit. Recreation and sports give exercise and teach teamwork, but when they become an obsession they rob time as our idols. Social media, internet surfing, computer games, and online entertainment easily devour spare minutes and even hours. Take spare moments to seek the things above in the midst of a busy day, maybe with the help of an app on your device or book beside your chair.

What we do when we do not "have to do" anything often betrays the priorities and preferences of our hearts. Haven't you found that your greatest problem in your use of time is your heart? What reason we have to confess to God our sin! How we need the cleansing blood of Christ and the righteous covering of the Savior, who always redeemed the time He received to work and rest. Let us seek His enlivening grace to lead us to set our affections on the things above and to give us true love to others.

God's grace enables us to enjoy His gifts with thankfulness to Him, redeem leisure time, and delight in the greatest recreation of all. The Puritan Isaac Ambrose wrote, "Contemplation is soul-recreation." He then proceeded to write a large volume (recommended reading!) entitled *Looking Unto Jesus*. As important as other uses of leisure time are, the most blessed activity involves seeking and delighting in the Lord. That is why God gave a weekly day of rest. Though we may not consider the Sabbath "leisure time," it is "time when one is not working." Guard that day, devote it to spiritual exercises, treasure the means of grace God gives on it, and seek rest in Christ. His grace makes this weekly day of rest the highlight of "leisure time" and will affect how you spend your spare moments and free days.

Witnessing for Christ

Christians are called to be witnesses of Christ in a sinful world. This calling is established by Christ's own command (Acts 1:8) as well as by the example of the post-Pentecost church. All saved sinners desire to share the gospel with others. But more than just an activity (e.g., evangelism), our new identity as believers includes being witnesses of Christ. We are witnesses at all times, even when we are not engaged in evangelism or other missional activities.

The word witness is a legal term. It designates a person who has a personal knowledge of an important reality and who is willing to make public testimony to the truth of that reality. To witness about something means to consistently profess its truth and give evidence that verifies this profession. Thus Christians are witnesses of Christ. They have a personal, experiential knowledge of Christ. They publicly testify of Christ's Lordship and gospel before all peoples. Their words and lifestyle—when living by grace—are verifiable evidence of the truth.

How should we live as witnesses? Christ set the perfect pattern for us, and then sent His Spirit to fill and equip us for this task. We, like Timothy, are to follow Christ's example: "I give thee charge in the sight of God… and before Christ Jesus, who before Pontius Pilate witnessed a good confession that thou keep this commandment without spot, unrebukeable" (1 Tim. 6:13–14).

Truth was on trial during the time of Pontius Pilate. Truth Incarnate stood before this Gentile judge. The evidence of Christ's life demanded a verdict, and the clear testimony was His innocence and His divinity. Truth was also on trial in the larger courtroom of the Jewish people and before all nations (cf. Isa. 43:8–12). Christ is "the faithful witness" (Rev. 1:5) who witnessed a "good confession." Likewise, every believer is called to faithful living in a way that is without reproach amid this sinful world (Matt. 5:16; Phil. 2:14–16; 1 Peter 2:12). As our Lord has been the faithful witness, so we are called to be His faithful witnesses.

How should we faithfully witness of Christ? A concise answer is impossible since most of the New Testament was written with the primary intent of instructing believers how to live as witnesses. But in short, living as a Christian witness means following Christ by displaying His character in this sinful world while declaring the truth of the gospel. Note the following practical considerations.

First, our witness is in the presence of the Father. Paul charges Timothy "in the sight of God" and, likewise, Christ promises to acknowledge faithful witnesses before the Father in heaven (Matt. 10:32). We often are tempted to evaluate our lives and activities by the judgment of others. It is easy to forget that our witness is, first of all, in the sight of God.

Second, our witness is before a world opposed to Christ and His truth. Be prepared to be misjudged and even mistreated, as was Christ, "who, when he was reviled, reviled not again; when he suffered, he threatened not; but committed himself to him that judgeth righteously" (1 Peter 2:23).

Third, we are to witness with loving conviction. Many people are headed heedlessly to an eternal hell. We must love them enough to be socially and politically incorrect, warning them of their spiritual danger and pointing them to Christ.

We who have personally experienced the reality of gospel transformation cannot but share this peace and joy with others (1 John 1:3–4).

Fourth, we are to witness with dignity, humility, and confidence in Christ who is the Truth. Think of Christ standing on trial before a wicked judge and devious religious leaders. Reflect on His regal dignity and the gentle majesty in which He displayed righteous living. Consider His gracious meekness and humility (Phil. 2:5–8). Here stands the King of the universe being mocked by wicked men; but He had willingly condescended in order to testify of God's amazing love to save sinners. Be encouraged by His quiet confidence. Truth was not determined by the outcome of Pilate's judgment; Christ was and is and will always be the Truth, and soon every tongue will confess it.

Defending Our Faith

"Defending the faith" is one definition of apologetics. However, defending the faith is not an academic exercise so much as the responsibility of every Christian. It is to be lived, not just studied. How? We read in 1 Peter 3:15, "But sanctify the Lord God in your hearts: and be ready always to give an answer to every man that asketh you a reason of the hope that is in you with meekness and fear."

First, we defend our faith when we honor the Lord in our hearts. We must fear and honor the Lord more than we fear and honor people or ideas. The Word of the Lord matters more than the words of men and women. The Bible says, "the word of the Lord endureth for ever" (1 Peter 1:25). When the gospel of our Lord changes our lives and then our relationships and communities, we are defending our faith. As William Edgar has pointed out, apologetics is relevant every day not because of our insights into our culture, but because of the good news of the gospel, which is always fresh and powerful. Living in obedience to Scripture is then living in defense of our faith.

Second, we can live defending our faith by living with hope. Peter, while writing to a persecuted and dispersed people, assumed Christians would be living with such hope that people would ask them how and why. Today this hope is contrary to the self-help and despair that most of the world lives with, because this hope is not in human change. This hope is certain faith in the revelation and resurrection of Jesus Christ, which brings with it the promise of a great inheritance. Christians can exult, "Blessed be the God and Father of our Lord Jesus Christ, which according to his abundant mercy hath begotten us again unto a lively hope by the resurrection of Jesus Christ from the dead" (1 Peter 1:3). This hope is central to what it means to live as a Christian.

Third, we live defending our faith when we are ready to give an answer. It may be answering those whom we engage in conversation, or more particularly, those who ask us why we have hope. We often think this will require much study and understanding of philosophy, culture, and other religions, and this knowledge is possible and helpful. But you do not need that before you begin defending your faith; Peter says be ready to give an answer for your hope, not your knowledge (1 Peter 1:13)! But are we living in conversation with others? Are we using creation, morality, desire, beauty, relationships, parenting, and eternity as topics of conversation with others where our hope (as informed by Scripture) can shine through? Are you ready to answer the questions: What do you believe? Why do you believe that?

Fourth, we defend our faith when we live with meekness and fear, or with gentleness and respect. As we defend ourselves, it is easy to begin to attack others. There may be a place for going on the offensive against ideas (2 Cor. 10:5), but we must remember we are not defending ourselves; we are defending the hope that we have in Christ. This must be done with winsomeness, a respectful attitude, and a good conscience. We must put away all malice, deceit, hypocrisy, envy, and all slander (1 Peter 2:1), even in the context of persecution and hatred.

However, it is how we must live as we defend our faith (1 Peter 2:13–19). "For it is better...that ye suffer for well doing, than for evil doing" (1 Peter 3:17).

For all four of these, we need the gift of the Holy Spirit in us so we can honor the Lord and live with hope (Rom. 15:13), as well as having Him work through us so that we can properly live and defend our faith (John 15:26). So, as you consider how you should defend the faith, think about your own life rather than others: Is your life honoring the Lord? Is your life shining with hope? Is your life ready to engage others? Is your life lived with gentleness and respect?

Facing Sickness and Death

Man is not naturally inclined to face sickness and death well. The unbeliever lives for the here and now, and this life is everything to him. He dreams of a life free of illness and adversity, even free of death. His life consists of the pursuit of happiness, and he would want to live here forever if that were attainable. The ungodly therefore respond in anger and bitterness when illness and/or death interrupts their pursuit of a vain happiness that so often eludes them.

If only it were true that Christians were free of such sinful emotions and such a sinful response to illness and death. When serious illness and the possibility of death suddenly intrude our lives, such a struggle arises in our hearts. The flesh can rear its ugly head when the prospect of chronic or terminal illness dramatically alters the course of our lives.

Such an unbecoming reaction to divinely sent affliction will, however, be a matter of grief to the believer, as it is the desire of his renewed inner man to surrender fully to the providential leadings of his heavenly Father. How intense the prayerful struggle to surrender wholeheartedly to a God who in His sovereign wisdom is slaying me in order to accomplish His purpose in my life!

And yet such wholehearted surrender alone will enable us to face the reality of illness or the inescapable prospect of death. Such surrender enabled Job to say that he would still trust the God who was slaying him and had thrust him into the furnace of affliction. "Though he slay me, yet will I trust in him" (Job 13:5). The grace of God prevailed mightily in a man who, on another occasion, cursed the day he was born.

Clearly, only the sustaining grace of God can enable us to face sickness and death as a Christian—that is, as someone who trusts his heavenly Father and the unfailing promises of His Word. We must learn to make use of these promises when serious trials become our portion. Only by appropriating God's precious covenantal promises will we be able to rise above our circumstances and trust our heavenly Father when nothing appears to make any sense. We must learn to judge God by His Word rather than our feelings and circumstances.

Such unwavering trust enabled Paul and Silas to sing God's praises when they found themselves in abysmal circumstances (Acts 16:22-24). Such trust enabled countless believers throughout the ages to remain steadfast during seasons of great trial. Christ wanted to teach His disciples this great lesson when He came to them in a raging storm. He first calmed their hearts by speaking to them before silencing the storm. His objective was to teach them (and us!) that in the midst of grievous trials, they should first consider His Word rather than circumstances. What are some of the promises we can prayerfully appropriate when facing sickness or death?

"Can a woman forget her sucking child, that she should not have compassion on the son of her womb? Yea, they may forget, yet will I not forget thee" (Isa. 49:15). Even when God leads us in ways that are far beyond our understanding, God cannot forget His own. His eye will always be upon those who fear Him.

"We know that all things work together for good to them that love God, to them who are the called according to his purpose" (Rom. 8:28). Even through sickness and death, God is working things together for the spiritual good of those who love Him, conforming them to the image of His Son (v. 29).

This is only a small sample of the many promises our heavenly Father wants us to appropriate by faith. What a blessing when God's grace enables us to say with the psalmist, "What time I am afraid, I will trust in thee. In God I will praise his word, in God I have put my trust" (Ps. 56:3–4)! Only by faith (a gracious gift of God) can we face sickness and death and echo the words of Psalm 112:7: "[I] shall not be afraid of evil tidings: [my] heart is fixed, trusting in the Lord."

Living Positively

We live in an increasingly negative culture in which it's easy to be dragged down with all the discouraging and depressing events that flood our hearts and overwhelm our minds. However, the apostle Paul calls us to enjoy God's peace in the midst of the storm by feeding our minds on an alternative media diet. He writes: "Finally, brethren, whatsoever things are true, whatsoever things are honest, whatsoever things are just, whatsoever things are pure, whatsoever things are lovely, whatsoever things are of good report; if there be any virtue, and if there be any praise, think on these things" (Phil. 4:8).

This is not an argument for unrealistic isolation from the bad news that inevitably fills a fallen world. No, this is a warrant, even a demand, that in our media choices we choose a deliberate imbalance in favor of what is inspirational and wholesome, instead of the current imbalance on the side of what is dispiriting and gross. Paul's "Food Pyramid" for a healthy media diet contains six main categories:

1. *True Not False*: Avoid listening to lies, misrepresentation, imbalance, and distortion, on both the left and the right of the political spectrum. Beware of journalists who spend most of their time exposing the lies of "the other team." Instead, seek out the most truthful, balanced, and fair reporting. Feast on truth, wherever it appears and whoever is speaking it. Surround yourself with truth-tellers rather than muck-spreaders.

2. *Noble Not Base*: The media tends to publicize the vile and sordid side of life. Their reporters and resources are

focused on the seedy cesspools of our society. "Don't do this to yourself!" appealed Paul. Trash the base and nourish the noble in your life. Noble means "majestic, awe-inspiring, worthy, and elevating": seek out media that elevate the heroic, that inspire awe, and that generate worship.

3. *Right Not Wrong*: When Paul says we should think about what is "just," he means what conforms to God's law and standards—right conduct in all of life. Paul urges us to seek out and celebrate right behavior, courageous actions, hardworking parents, loving fathers, devoted mothers, respectful children, happy families, gentle caregivers, honest employees, fair bosses, etc.

4. *Pure Not Filthy*: When was the last time you saw a film that celebrated Christian marriage or portrayed a normal functioning family? Immorality, abuse, fighting, and murder rule the day. Take the steps to move the spotlight to happy and godly relationships, long and faithful marriages, etc. Rejoice over the many godly young people who do not use porn, who do not dress immodestly, who keep their hearts with all diligence, and who keep themselves pure for marriage.

5. *Beautiful Not Ugly*: "Whatsoever things are lovely" describes what is attractive and winsome, words and actions that compel admiration and affection. In a day when many of us live among steel and concrete boxes of varying sizes and shapes, it's often very difficult to locate beauty in our immediate surroundings. We need to get out of the city, see the stunning mountains, savor the fragrance of the forest, taste the thrill of fresh and healthy produce, and listen to the exquisite birdsong. Find ways to increase your intake of beauty through your various senses.

6. *Praising Not Complaining*: Paul was saying, "Focus on what is constructive rather than destructive." Feast on whatever makes people exclaim "Well done!" rather than what makes you and others say, "That's terrible." As you drive with your family, do you suggest topics that will show people in a good light or in a bad light? Do you tell stories that will make your hearers praise God and others or in a way that will make people doubt God and condemn others?

As Paul puts it in his summary of these six criteria, "If there be any virtue, and if there be any praise, think on these things" (v. 8). This was not just a theory for Paul; he could appeal to their memory of him: "Those things, which ye have both learned, and received, and heard, and seen in me, do: and the God of peace shall be with you" (Phil. 4:9). He says, if you think like I think and do what I do, you will replace fear, anxiety, depression, and worry with divine peace.

Living for God's Glory

What a lofty goal this is! What could be higher? Yet this is the chief end of everyone who has ever lived. God deserves all glory due to His name (Ps. 29:2). He says it Himself: "This people have I formed for myself, they shall shew forth my praise" (Isa. 43:21). The happiest beings are the angels and glorified saints in heaven, who glorify God eternally. Paul put it this way: "Ye are redeemed with a price, therefore glorify God in your body, and in your spirit" (1 Cor. 6:20).

First, we must be redeemed by Christ. By nature, we come short of the glory of God; in fact, we are enemies of it (Rom. 1:21–23; 3:23). We deserve everlasting shame because we have not glorified God rightly. We must be redeemed. Our service to sin must end, and Christ's blood and righteousness must be applied to set us free from the penalty and power of sin (Gal. 3:13–14; 5:24). He lived a perfect life that glorified God without fail; He paid the full ransom price on Calvary. Are you redeemed by His precious blood? Without this great Redeemer, you are lost and will never attain the purpose for which you were made.

Second, we must glorify God in our bodies. Many in the Corinthian church were returning to their former fleshly sins. The body is not for fornication (1 Cor. 6:13), but for the Lord. "Know ye not that your body is the temple of the Holy Ghost?" (1 Cor. 6:19). There is a great dignity to our bodies. They are not a garbage dump. They are temples of the Holy Ghost. Therefore glorify God in your body.

Let us use our eyes rightly, as Jesus did, who was filled with compassion as He looked on the multitude. Let our ears turn away from the voices of the world and use them to listen to God's Word and the advice of the godly, even if it is reproof. Let us use our lips not for gossip, but to pray, to speak of the Lord Jesus, and to speak comfort to the downcast. Let us use our hands not to steal, but to work diligently, and to give for the good of others (Eph. 4:28). Let us use our feet to go to the house of God, to walk in His ways, and to follow the Lord Jesus in His footsteps (1 Peter 2:21).

Third, we must glorify God in our spirit. Let us think high thoughts of God, read His Word, and submit to His will. Let us trust in Him, as was said of Abram: "he was strong in faith ... giving glory to God" (Rom. 4:20). Let us give glory to God by confessing our sins, as David acknowledging his sin and justifying God (Ps. 51). Let us give glory to God by a life of holiness, being made conformable to His Son, denying ourselves, and taking up our cross. Let us give glory to God by being thankful, as the leper who returned to Jesus to render thanks to Him (Luke 17:18). This is our reasonable service, isn't it (Rom. 12:1)?

He has bought you with His precious blood, so glorify Him in your body and in your soul. How sad when common activities like eating and drinking remain only common activities!

That is how they lived in Noah's days, swallowing it all down without honoring the Giver of these gifts. But Paul says that the children of God should be marked by doing everything to His glory (1 Cor. 10:31).

The secret? The favorable presence of God. That was the secret to Joseph's life of glorifying God in trying times. He was far from his parents, far from the Promised Land, but the Lord was not far from him. God was with him (Gen.

39:2). He experienced the communion and nearness of the Lord. Can we do with less?

Let us look to the Savior from God who could say, "I have glorified thee on the earth: I have finished the work which thou gavest me to do" (John 17:4). He gives His Spirit in answer to your prayer: "Help me thy will to do."

Finally, let us never forget that living for God's glory will, by grace, end one day in living in God's glory with Jesus Christ forever, together with the redeemed made perfect and the holy angels. There, dear believer, as a perfect bride, you will be in a utopian marriage with your perfect Bridegroom, living to the glory of the triune God forever. "He which testifieth these things saith, Surely I come quickly. Amen. Even so, come, Lord Jesus. The grace of our Lord Jesus Christ be with you all. Amen" (Rev. 22:20-21).